Collins

Tree of Life 2

A Course on Environmental Studies

Dinu Raheja
Lipika Ghosh

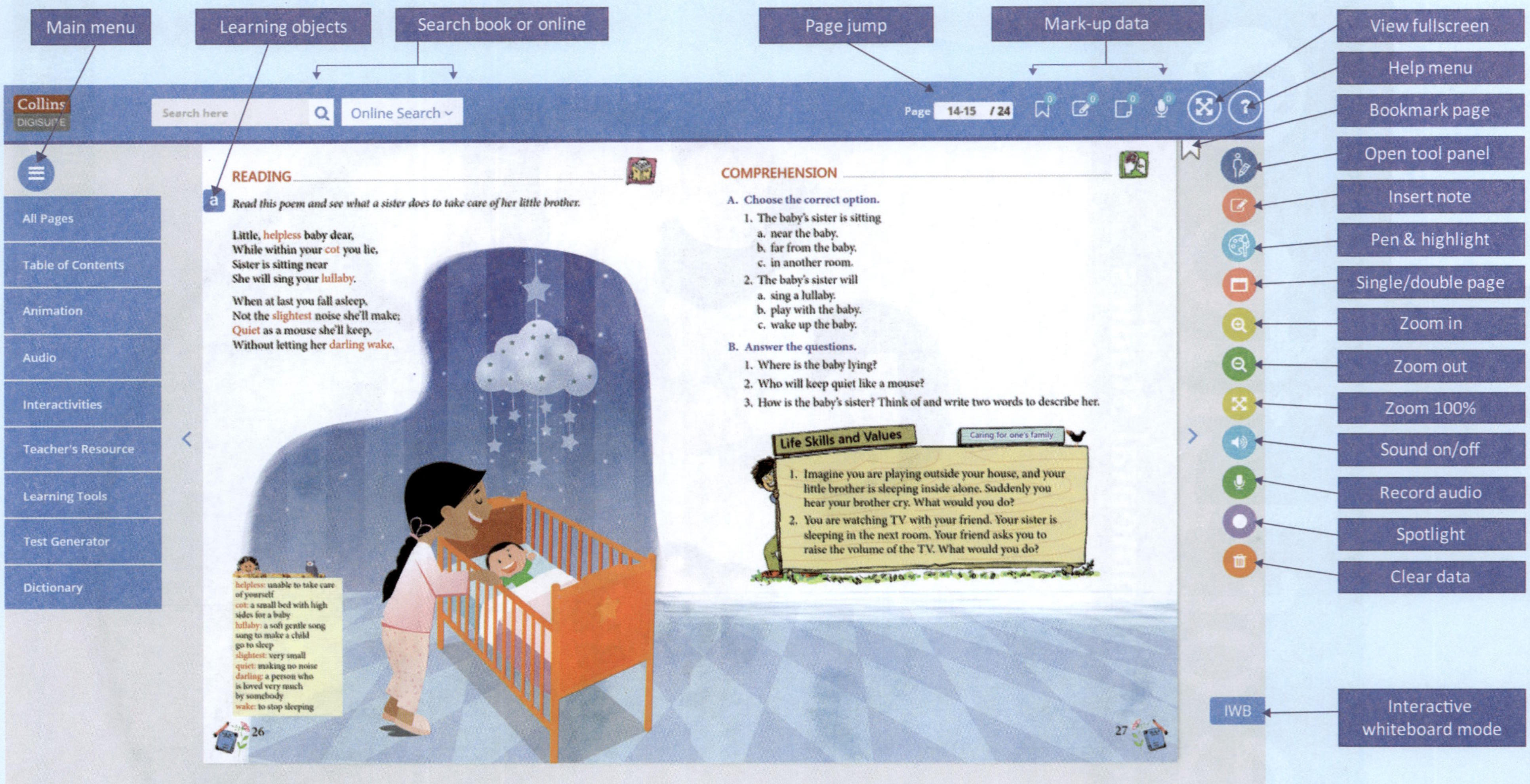

Student + Teacher		Teacher-only	
a animations	ia activities	g games	lp lesson plans	tn teacher's notes

Student + Teacher

- **a** animations
- **ia** activities
- **g** games
- **ilt** instructor-led tutorials
- **w** worksheets
- **v** videos
- audio

Teacher-only

- **lp** lesson plans
- **tn** teacher's notes
- **w** worksheets
- **ak** answer keys

Preface

Tree of Life Updated Edition is an engaging and innovative course on Environmental Studies for classes 1 to 5. It adopts a multidisciplinary approach to ensure holistic learning for young learners. This series of five books adheres to the National Education Policy, 2020. An interactive and learner-centric course, *Tree of Life* has planned pedagogical elements that help learners connect social, cultural and scientific concepts with real-life situations. Promoting experiential learning, learners are encouraged to explore their immediate world and foster environmental awareness. The well-graded content has been created keeping in mind several goals—easy readability, accuracy and creativity. At the same time it empowers learners towards higher levels of academic scholarship.

The concepts in the series are presented simply, supplemented by colourful pictures and illustrations. Varied key features in the series hone learning skills.

- Multidisciplinary and a holistic education—**Exploration Station, Cross connect**
- Life skills and making ethical decisions—**Learn the ropes**
- Creativity, art integration, creating joyful classrooms—**Put your heads together**
- Organic living—**Poster, United Nations Sustainability Development Goals**
- A rootedness and pride in India—**Our Heritage**
- Inquiry-based, discovery-based, discussion-based, and analysis-based learning—**Get the ball rolling, Clued in, Give it a shot**
- Application and problem-solving—**Think through, Covid-19 Safety**
- Exploratory activities and experiential learning—**Why it Works**
- Moving towards real understanding and towards learning how to learn—**Wrap up**
- Assessment—**Brush up**

It is our endeavour to help the learners develop a responsible attitude towards the preservation of their environment.

- Authors

About the authors

Dinu Raheja, an innovative educationist and administrator, recipient of the International Teacher's Award, has over 15 years of teaching experience in Indian and international schools. Formerly, Middle School Incharge, Sanskriti School, New Delhi, she is currently Program Director with The Global Education & Leadership Foundation (tGELF). Dinu also facilitates teacher leadership development workshops.

Lipika Ghosh has over 25 years of teaching experience at St. Xavier's School Hazaribagh, Sardar Patel Vidyalaya, New Delhi and Sanskriti School, New Delhi. She has used innovative teaching methodology to make science a process of discovery interspersed with anecdotes for learners. Lipika has taught analytical skills and inculcated awareness of social issues amongst learners through science.

Key Features

Tree of Life Updated Edition is an engaging and innovative course on Environmental Studies for classes 1 to 5. The series adheres to the National Education Policy, 2020 and adopts a multidisciplinary approach to enable holistic learning.

Get the ball rolling has compelling pre-teaching warm-up tasks to arouse interest in the topic.

Give it a shot promotes experiential learning through application-based activities.

Think through provides referencing tasks to develop critical thinking skills of the learners.

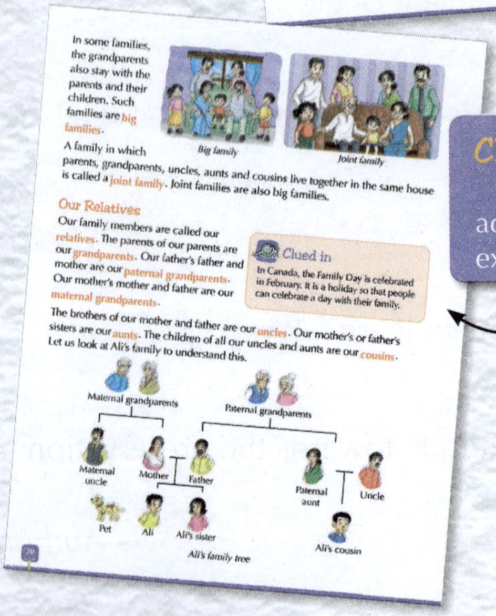

Clued in provides interesting additional facts for extended learning.

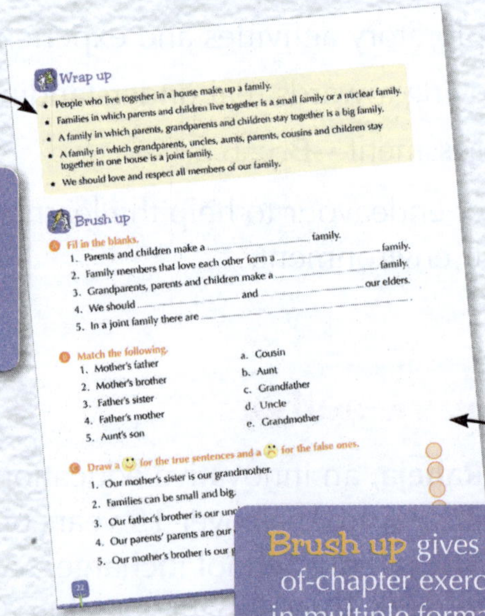

Wrap up provides a ready reckoner to reinforce the concepts taught for comprehensive learning.

Brush up gives end-of-chapter exercises in multiple formats to facilitate assessment.

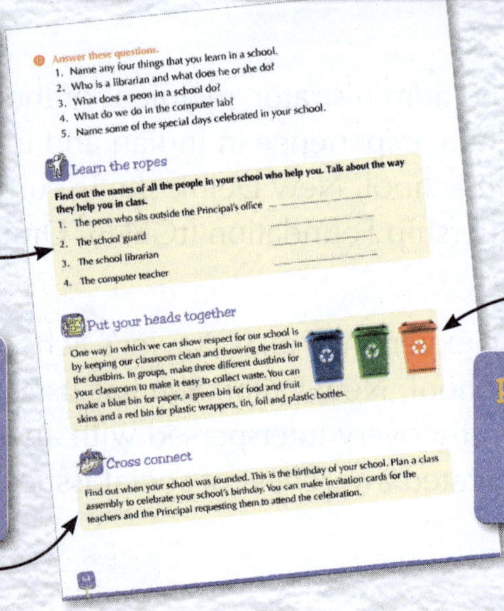

Learn the ropes provides activities for application of 21st century life skills.

Put your heads together provides group projects to strengthen teamwork and cooperative learning.

Cross connect tasks promote cross-disciplinary and integrated learning.

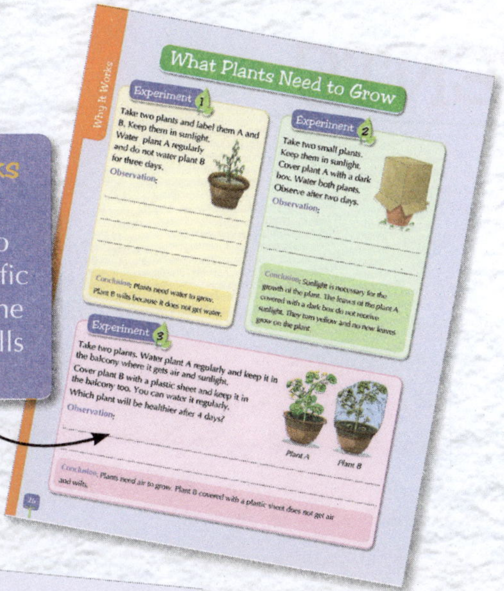

Why It Works provides experiments to promote scientific temper and hone observation skills of learners.

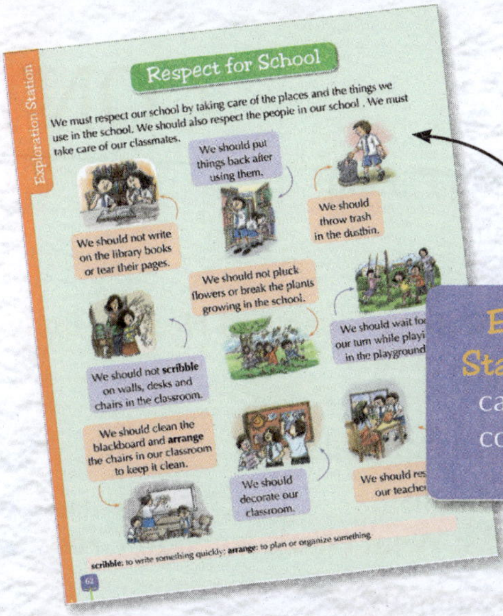

Exploration Station provides case studies for comprehensive knowledge.

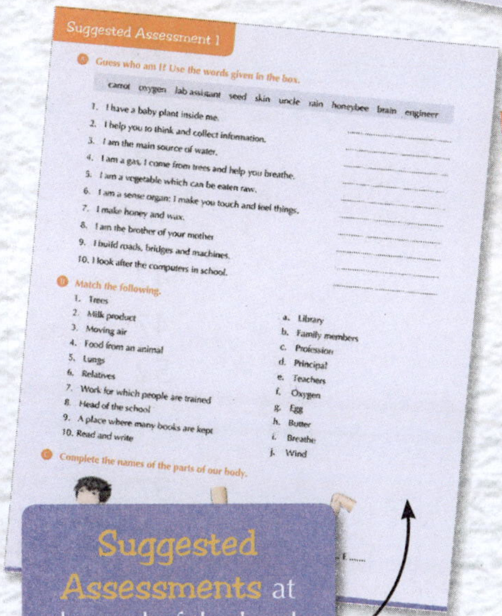

Suggested Assessments at the end of the book facilitate cumulative assessment.

Covid-19 Safety teaches students to stay safe and healthy.

Our Heritage provides snippets of information about the heritage of India and encourages learners to preserve it.

United Nations Sustainability Development Goals featured in specific sections to achieve a just and equitable world for all.

Poster on 5Rs sensitizes learners towards their surroundings and creates awareness about sustainability of the environment.

CONTENTS

1 About Myself

Get the ball rolling

Look at these pictures. Talk about them in class.

Write about yourself.

1. My name is ....
2. My birthday is on ....
3. I live with my ....
4. My mother's name is ....
5. My father's name is ....

Draw or paste your picture here.

Growing Up

We grow older with every birthday. As we grow older, our body changes. We become bigger, taller and we start doing many things we could not do when we were younger. Our old clothes and shoes become small for us. This is known as **growing up**.

Growing up

Give it a shot

Complete these sentences.

1. I am .... years old now.
2. I have .... sister/brother.
3. My height is ....
4. My weight is ....
5. My shoe size is ....

As we grow older, we learn new things. We can do many tasks on our own. Look at these tasks and tick (✓) the ones that you can do.

1.  ☐ I can read a book.
2.  ☐ I can ride a bike.
3.  ☐ I can tie my shoelaces.
4.  ☐ I can brush my teeth.

Clued in

Growing children must have good sleeping habits. Sleeping well gives us energy and helps our body grow.

We are Special

Look around your class. Are all children the same? No, they are not. Every child looks **different** from each other. Each one likes different things. Each one is **special**.

Playing games is a hobby

A **hobby** is an activity that we like to do in our free time. Different people have different hobbies. The things that we like become our favourite things. We feel differently too. Some things make us happy and some things make us sad.

different: not the same as another or each other; **special:** different from others

Write your favourite things.

- Colour ....
- Storybook ....
- Game ....

Think through

Whom will you call when you need help? Find out your parent's phone numbers and write them down.

My mother's phone number ....

My father's phone number ....

Wrap up

- We grow older with every birthday.
- As we grow older, we learn new things.
- Each one of us is special.
- A hobby is an activity we like to do in our free time.
- The things we like become our favourite things.

Brush up

A Fill in the blanks with words you have learnt.

1. The day we are born is our .... (myday/birthday)
2. The thing I like to do in my free time is my .... (hobby/activity)
3. The thing I like is my .... thing. (special/favourite)
4. I am ...., and I am different from others. (special/usual)

B Tick (✓) the correct answers.

1. This does not change when we grow up
   a. weight b. height c. name
2. This changes every year
   a. birthday b. age c. name
3. Things we can do on our own
   a. cross the road b. iron our clothes c. read a storybook
4. This makes us sad
   a. music b. fighting c. games

5. When we grow older we become
   a. weaker   b. smaller   c. stronger

C **Name two fruits and two vegetables you love to eat.**

....

D **Answer these questions.**

1. Which school do you go to?
2. Who is your best friend?
3. Name the town or city you live in.
4. What is a hobby?

Learn the ropes

Talk to your grandparents. Name some of their favourite things.

- Colour ....
- Book ....
- Food ....
- Place ....
- Dress ....
- Movie ....

Put your heads together

In pairs, grow a plant in class and give a name to it. Learn how to take care of the plant and take turns to water it regularly. You can ask your teacher for help.

Cross connect

Write a few lines about yourself in your notebook and paste or draw some of your pictures.

2 Our Body

Get the ball rolling

How do you feel when you run a lot? Do you like to play games in the park?

When we look in the mirror, we can see the different parts of our body. Different parts of our body do different things. They all work together so that we can eat, sit, play, study and sleep.

Each part of our body that carries out a particular function is known as an **organ**. The three types of organs are **external organs**, **sense organs** and **internal organs**.

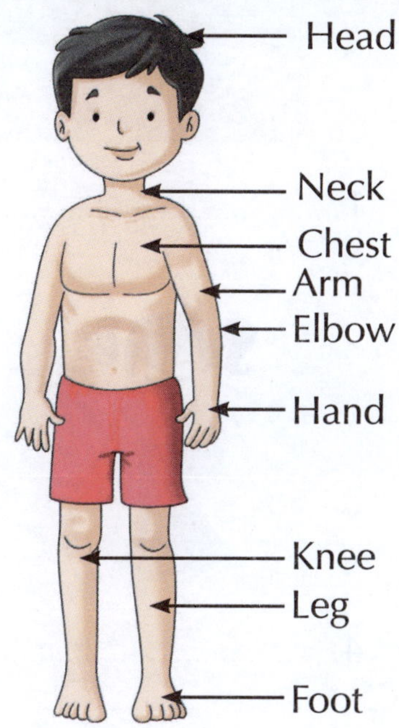

External organs

External Organs

The parts of the body that can be seen and are outside the body are called **external organs**. Our head, neck, arms, elbow, chest, hands, legs and feet are external organs. Arms and legs are also called **limbs**. They help us do many things.

Sense Organs

The parts of the body that help us feel and **sense** things around us are known as **sense organs**. We have five sense organs. They are eyes, ears, nose, tongue and skin. They help us to see, hear, smell, taste and feel.

A pair of **eyes** helps us to see things around us.

A pair of **ears** helps us to hear sounds.

The **nose** helps us to smell and breathe.

The **tongue** helps us to taste sweet, sour, salty and bitter things. It also helps us to speak.

The **skin** helps us to touch and feel things.

Clued in

Our body is made up of bones and muscles. All the bones in the body together form the **skeleton**. Muscles are the soft parts of our body.

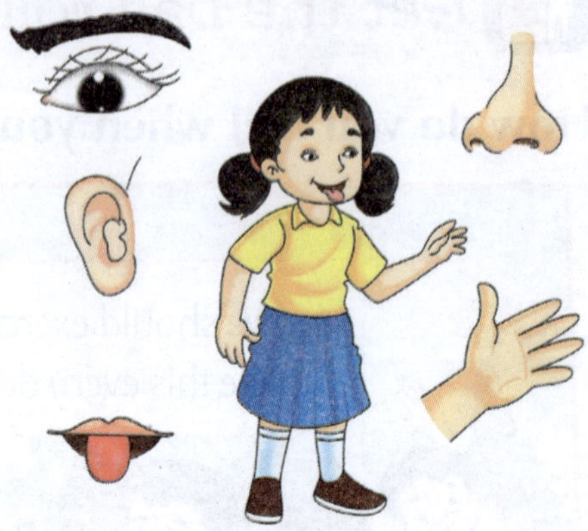

Sense organs

Give it a shot

Name the parts of the body that are being used to perform the actions in these pictures.

1. ....

2. ....

3. ....

4. ....

5. ....

6. ....

sense: the physical abilities of sight, smell, hearing, touch and taste

Clean and Healthy Body

We must keep our body clean and healthy. To stay healthy, we must follow some **good habits**.

Sleep for at least 8 to 9 hours every day.

Wake up early in the morning and go to sleep early.

Brush our teeth every morning and at night before going to bed.

Bathe every day.

Change our clothes every day and wear neat and clean clothes.

Wash and comb our hair to keep it tidy.

Wash our hands before and after eating our meals.

Eat healthy food.

Exercise every day.

Play in a park every day.

Internal Organs

The parts of the body that are inside and cannot be seen are called **internal organs**. Some internal organs are brain, heart, lungs and stomach.

The **brain** is inside the head. It helps us to think and collect information from our surroundings. It sends signals to all parts of the body to work. The **heart** is inside the chest. It pumps blood to all parts of the body. It beats continuously. The sound of the **heartbeat** is lub-dub-lub-dub. A pair of **lungs** is inside the chest. Lungs help us to breathe. The air we breathe in enters through our nose into the lungs. The **stomach** is inside the belly. The food from the mouth goes into the stomach. It helps us to **digest** the food.

Think through

Which part of the body makes us laugh or cry?

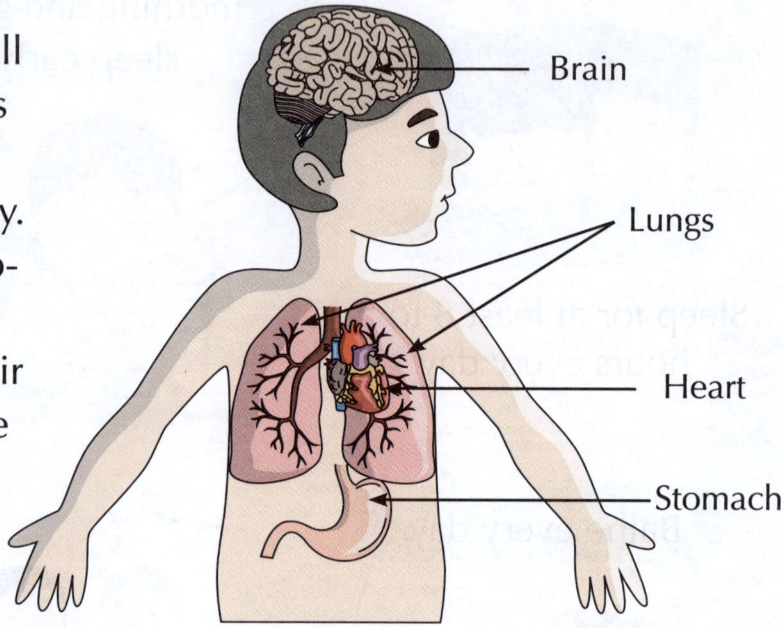

Internal organs

Wrap up

* Our body is made up of different parts like head, chest, hands, legs and feet.
* Our body has external organs, sense organs and internal organs.
* The parts of the body that we can see and are outside our body are called external organs.
* The parts of the body that help us to feel and sense things are known as sense organs.
* The parts of the body that are inside our body and we cannot see are called internal organs.
* We must keep our body clean and healthy.

digest: the process by which food is broken down inside the stomach

Brush up

A Look at the pictures and fill in the missing letters to name different parts of the body.

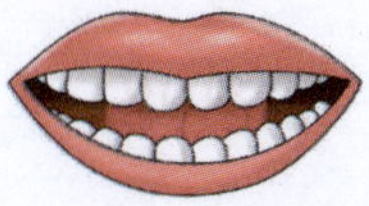

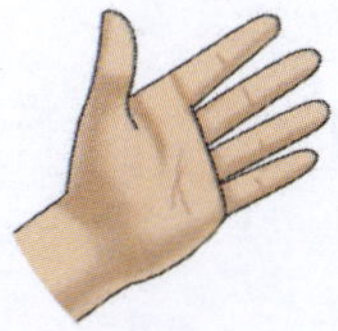

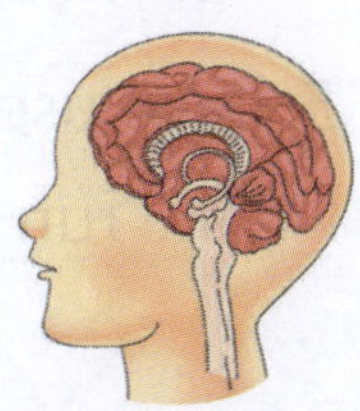

1. T .... T H 2. F .... G .... S 3. ...... R .... N

B Find the names of 10 different parts of the body hidden in this word grid. Use different colours to highlight them. One has been done for you.

A	L	U	N	G	S	L	O	W	R	H
S	T	O	M	A	C	H	R	S	E	A
E	L	B	O	W	T	A	G	E	D	N
N	O	T	A	L	W	D	N	K	O	D
E	S	A	Y	B	R	A	I	N	N	S
C	P	R	E	O	I	R	F	E	E	T
K	A	M	I	W	F	P	A	E	A	R
O	C	H	E	S	T	E	C	S	L	Y

C Tick (✓) the correct answers.

1. The food we eat goes from the mouth to the

   a. brain b. stomach c. hands d. legs

2. The part of the body that pumps blood

   a. lungs b. stomach c. heart d. brain

3. An internal organ

a. brain b. head c. chest d. knee

4. The brain collects information from

a. nose b. eyes c. ears d. all of these

5. We use our fingers to

a. run b. jump c. write d. sing

D Answer these questions.

1. Name five external organs.
2. Name the internal organs of the body.
3. How do you keep your body clean?

Learn the ropes

Tick (✓) the actions that you should do and cross (✗) those that you should not do to take care of your body.

1. Exercise daily ☐
2. Never brush your teeth ☐
3. Rub eyes often ☐
4. Take rest ☐
5. Clean the tongue ☐
6. Eat unhealthy food often ☐

Put your heads together

Form three groups in class. Members of the first group can take turns naming a body part. Members of the second group should try to spell the names of those body parts. The third group can explain their functions.

Cross connect

Take a chart paper. Place your favourite soft toy on it. Make an outline of its body with a crayon. Ask an adult to help you make a cut-out of the outline. Label its body parts and colour the picture. Show it to your friends in class.

3 My Family and I

Get the ball rolling

How many members are there in your family? Do you live with your parents and grandparents? Tell your teacher about your family.

People who live together in a house make up a **family**. Families can be of different sizes. Some families are small and some are big.

Big and Small Families

A family in which parents and their children live together is called a **small family** or a **nuclear family**.

Nuclear family

Single-parent family

There are some families in which children live only with one of their parents. These are **single-parent families**. Single-parent families are also small families.

In some families, the grandparents also stay with the parents and their children. Such families are **big families**.

Big family

Joint family

A family in which parents, grandparents, uncles, aunts and cousins live together in the same house is called a **joint family**. Joint families are also big families.

Our Relatives

Our family members are called our **relatives**. The parents of our parents are our **grandparents**. Our father's father and mother are our **paternal grandparents**. Our mother's mother and father are our **maternal grandparents**.

> **Clued in**
>
> In Canada, Family Day is celebrated in February. It is a holiday so that people can celebrate a day with their family.

The brothers of our mother and father are our **uncles**. Our mother's or father's sisters are our **aunts**. The children of all our uncles and aunts are our **cousins**. Let us look at Ali's family to understand this.

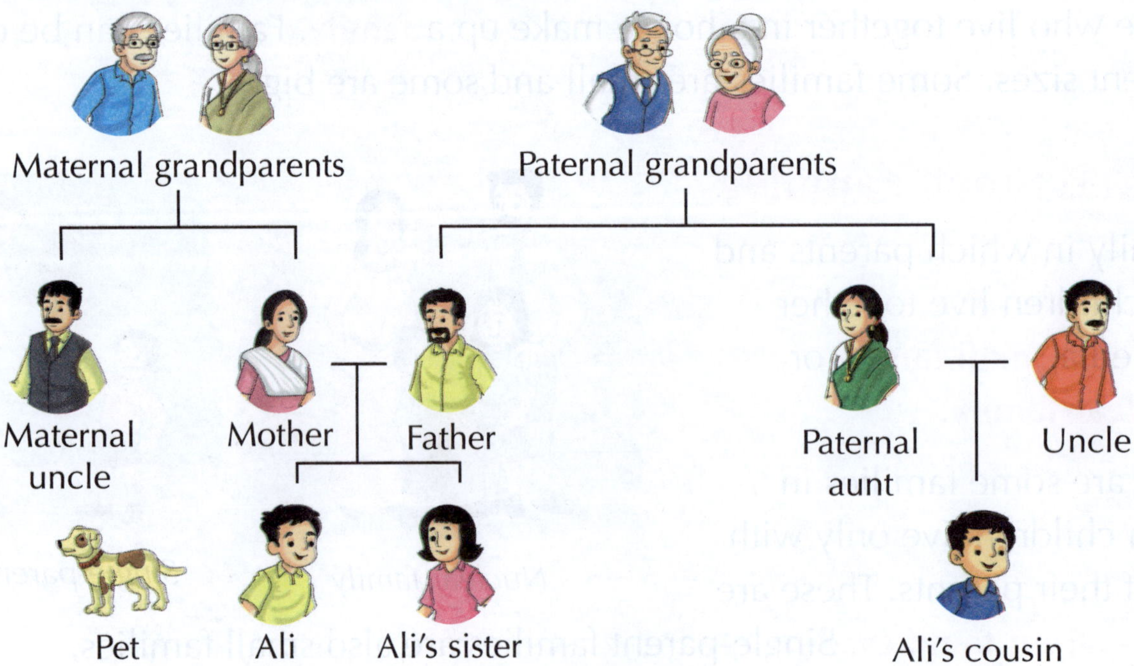

Ali's family tree

Give it a shot

Paste or draw pictures and write names of your family members to complete your family tree.

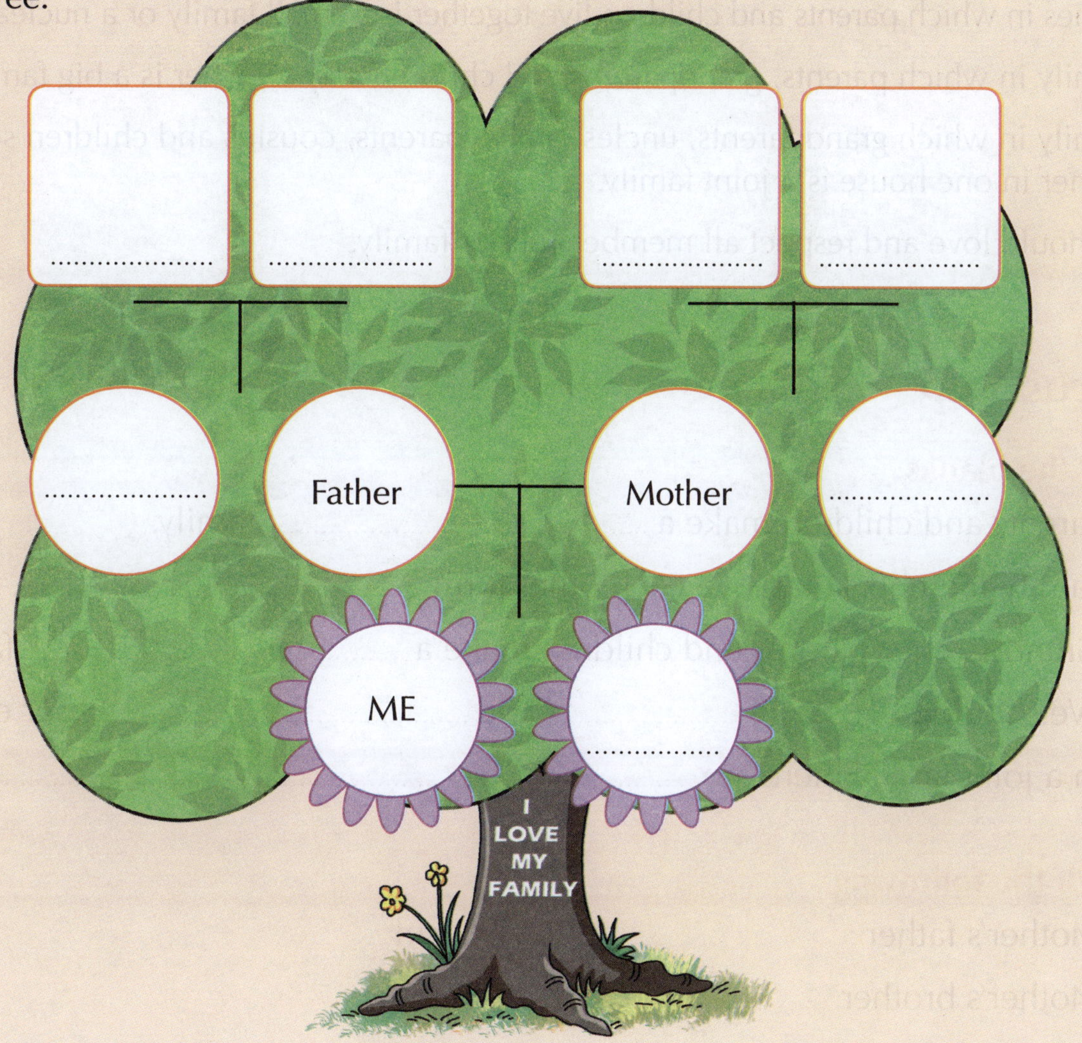

A Happy Family

Family members that love each other form a happy family. Everyone in the family should help and love each other. Our parents and grandparents look after us in many ways. We too should take care of our family by helping our parents and grandparents around the house. We celebrate special occasions with our entire family.

Think through

How do you help your family at home?

Family members help each other

Wrap up

- People who live together in a house make up a family.
- Families in which parents and children live together is a small family or a nuclear family.
- A family in which parents, grandparents and children stay together is a big family.
- A family in which grandparents, uncles, aunts, parents, cousins and children stay together in one house is a joint family.
- We should love and respect all members of our family.

Brush up

A Fil in the blanks.

1. Parents and children make a .... family.
2. Family members that love each other form a .... family.
3. Grandparents, parents and children make a .... family.
4. We should .... and .... our elders.
5. In a joint family there are ....

B Match the following.

1. Mother's father	a. Cousin
2. Mother's brother	b. Aunt
3. Father's sister	c. Grandfather
4. Father's mother	d. Uncle
5. Aunt's son	e. Grandmother

C Draw a ☺ for the true sentences and a ☹ for the false ones.

1. Our mother's sister is our grandmother.
2. Families can be small and big.
3. Our father's brother is our uncle.
4. Our parents' parents are our cousins.
5. Our mother's father is our grandfather.

D Answer these questions.

1. What is the difference between a nuclear family and a joint family?
2. How is a big family different from a joint family?
3. How do our grandparents show their love for us?
4. What is a happy family?
5. Who are our cousins?

Learn the ropes

Tick (✓) the things that you do to help your family at home.

Put your heads together

Do you share your toys, books or clothes with your friends and family? In groups, make a list of all the things you share with your friends, brother or sister. Draw or paste pictures of the things you share.

Cross connect

Make a family album of all the special occasions you have spent with your grandparents and other family members. Below each picture, write the date and the name of the occasion.

4 More About Plants

Get the ball rolling

How are plants important to us? Discuss this in class.

There are different types of plants around us. Some plants are big and some are small.

Types of Plants

Big plants with huge wooden stems are called **trees**. Some examples of trees are banyan tree, apple tree and coconut tree. Small plants with woody stems are **shrubs**. Some examples of shrubs are rose and hibiscus. Very small plants with soft stems are called **herbs**. Some examples of herbs are tulsi and mint.

Tulsi

Hibiscus

Banyan tree

Some plants have weak stems and need support to stand. They are called **climbers**. Some examples of climbers are bitter gourd, pea plant and grapevine. Some plants have weak stems and grow along the ground. They are called **creepers**. Some examples of creepers are pumpkin, muskmelon and watermelon.

Pumpkin

Pea plant

Parts of a Plant

Plants have many different parts. Each part has its own function.

Roots grow under the ground. They fix the plant in the soil. Roots take in water and minerals from the soil.

The **stem** grows above the soil. It bears leaves, flowers and fruits. It carries food and water to all parts of the plant.

Leaves make food for the plant. They are mostly green in colour. Green leaves make food in the presence of sunlight, air, water and minerals.

Flowers have different sizes, shapes, colours and scents. They grow from **buds**. Some flowers change into **fruits**.

Fruits grow on plants that have flowers. Some fruits can be eaten and some should not be eaten.

Seeds are present inside the fruit. They have a baby plant inside them. The seeds, when planted back into the soil and receive the right amount of water, air and sunlight, grow into a new plant.

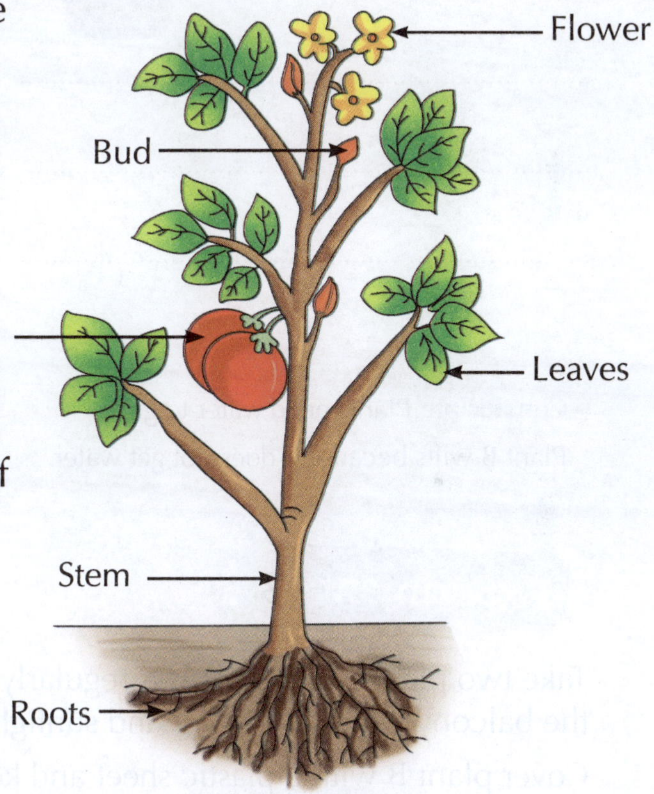

Parts of a plant

Clued in

Green leaves use water, minerals, sunlight and carbon dioxide and turn it into food. This process is called photosynthesis.

What Plants Need to Grow

Experiment 1

Take two plants and label them A and B. Keep them in sunlight. Water plant A regularly but do not water plant B for three days.

Observation:

....

....

....

Conclusion: Plants need water to grow. Plant B wilts because it does not get water.

Experiment 2

Take two small plants. Keep them in sunlight. Cover plant A with a cardboard box. Water both plants. Observe after two days.

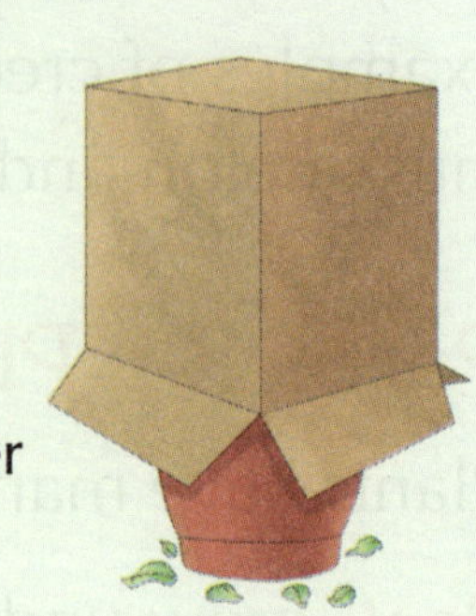

Observation:

....

....

Conclusion: Sunlight is necessary for the growth of the plant. The leaves of plant A covered with a cardboard box, do not receive sunlight. They turn yellow and no new leaves grow on the plant.

Experiment 3

Take two plants. Water plant A regularly and keep it in the balcony where it gets air and sunlight.

Cover plant B with a plastic sheet and keep it in the balcony too. You can water it regularly.

Which plant will be healthier after 4 days?

Plant A *Plant B*

Observation:

....

....

Conclusion: Plants need air to grow. Plant B covered with a plastic sheet does not get air and wilts.

Uses of Plants

Plants provide us:

- vegetables, fruits and **cereals** or **food grains**.
- medicines and spices.
- oil and perfumes.
- wood, which is used for making furniture.
- oxygen to breathe.
- food for some animals.

Give it a shot

Observe four fruits—banana, mango, apple and orange. Which of these fruits have seeds? Plant seeds of any one fruit and water it regularly for a month. Can you see tiny plants growing from the seeds?

Things we get from plants

Think through

Why do leaves make food only during the day?

cereals: food grains like wheat and rice

Wrap up

* Plants are of different types—trees, shrubs, herbs, climbers and creepers.
* The different parts of a plant are roots, stem, leaves, buds, flowers and fruits.
* Leaves make food for the plant.
* New plants grow from seeds.
* Plants provide us with many useful things.

Brush up

A **Match the following.**

1. 
2. 
3. 
4. 
5. 

a. Makes food

b. Grows under ground

c. Contains seeds

d. Grows above the soil

e. Change into fruits

B **Tick (✓) the correct sentences and cross (×) the wrong ones.**

1. Roots make food for the plant.
2. Plants with weak stems that need support are called climbers.
3. Plants give us oils and medicines.
4. All leaves are green in colour.
5. All fruits can be eaten.

C **Fill in the blanks with the correct answers.**

1. Plants with weak stems that grow along the ground are called .... (climbers/creepers)
2. .... are part of the plant that grow from buds and change into fruits. (Leaves/Flowers)
3. Plants with woody stems are called .... (shrubs/herbs)
4. The .... takes in water and minerals from the soil. (stem/root)
5. Plants give us .... (shade/sunlight)

D **Answer these questions.**

1. Name the parts of a plant and write one function of each.
2. How are plants useful to us?
3. How do leaves make food for the plant?
4. How do seeds grow into new plants?

Learn the ropes

Imagine you are a plant and someone wants to adopt you. Make a list of instructions for your new owner, explaining how he or she should care for you.

Put your heads together

Form five groups in class. Each group can prepare an album on different parts of a plant. Write the name of five different kinds of plants which grow in your surroundings. Observe the following features of the plants:

- Stem: hard, soft, green, woody, thin, broad
- Leaves: colour, shape, texture, size
- Flowers: colour, size, fragrance
- Fruits: one seed, many seeds
- Seeds: big, small

Collect some of these parts of plants and let them dry. Paste the dried parts of plants in your scrapbook.

Cross connect

1. Recite this poem in class.

   A plant has a stem, and a root,
   Leaves of the plant make their food.
   It has flowers, which turn into fruit.
   Fruit protects the seed,
   which the plant needs.
   The seed has the baby plant inside,
   Which grows into a new plant,
   when it gets air, water and sunlight.

2. Pick up five fallen leaves and flowers. Dry them by placing them in thick books. Make greeting cards using drawing sheets and decorate them with dry flowers and colours.

5 More About Animals

Get the ball rolling

Can tiger cubs live with us in our homes? Talk about this in class.

Animals are found everywhere—some live on land, some live in water and some live both on land and in water.

Types of Animals

We have already learnt about wild animals, domestic animals and pets.

Wild animals are animals that live in forests or caves. These animals do not like being around human beings. Lions, tigers, leopards and giraffes are some wild animals.

Lion

Tiger

Giraffe

Domestic animals are animals that live with us usually on a farm. They help us do different types of work. Horses, cows and goats are some common domestic animals.

Cow

Goat

Horse

Pets are animals that live with us in our houses to give us company. They are our friends. Dogs, cats and rabbits are some common pet animals.

Rabbit

Dog

Cat

Food Animals Eat

Different animals eat different types of food. Animals like elephants, giraffes, horses, cows and goats eat grass, stems and leaves. They are known as **plant-eating animals**.

Animals like lions, tigers, leopards, foxes and owls eat the flesh of other animals. They are known as **flesh-eating animals**.

There are some animals that eat **both** plants as well as the flesh of other animals. Some of these animals are bears, squirrels, mice and raccoons.

Animals grow

When we get a new pet dog, it is small just like a baby and is called a puppy. Then it grows into a dog. All animals have babies.

A puppy grows into a dog

Animal Movements

Animals move from one place to another in search of food and **shelter**. Different animals move in different ways. Animals can run, walk, jump, hop, swim, fly, crawl or **glide**.

Clued in

Elephants are the only animals that cannot jump.

shelter: a place for living and protecting oneself from danger; **glide:** to move smoothly

Animals like lions, cheetahs, elephants, camels, and horses can walk and run. Kangaroos and rabbits hop. Earthworms and snakes move by pushing their bodies along the ground.

Cheetah

Horse

Elephant

Birds and some insects fly with the help of wings. Fish swim in water with the help of their **fins**.

Bird

Fish

Rabbit

Kangaroo

Give it a shot

In your notebook, write the name of one wild animal and one domestic animal. Draw a table and write the type of animal it is, the name of its home and the food it eats. Paste the pictures of these animals and write how they help us.

Animals Help Us

Animals are useful to us in many ways.

Cows, buffaloes and goats give us milk. We make curd, butter, ghee and cheese from milk. Hens, ducks and geese give us eggs. We get meat from animals like goat and chicken. Fish, crab and prawn are also eaten as seafood. We get honey and wax from bees.

Hens give us eggs

Cows give us milk

Bees give us honey and wax

fin: a thin flat part that sticks out from the body of a fish, used for swimming

Wool is obtained from the hair that covers the body of animals like sheep, goats, yaks and rabbits. Leather shoes, jackets, belts and bags are made from the skin of animals.

Animals like oxen, help to **plough** fields, **thresh** grains and draw out water from the well.

Yak

Oxen help to plough fields

Horses, camels, ponies and elephants are used as a means of transport. They also carry heavy loads.

Think through

Which animals are used to travel in hilly areas? Find out why.

Taking Care of Animals

We should be kind to animals and take care of them in the following ways:

- We should never tease animals or be cruel to them.
- If an animal is hurt or injured, we should ask an adult to help us to take it to a **veterinary doctor** or a vet.
- We should bathe our pets regularly and keep them clean.
- We should keep a clean bowl of water for birds and animals in the garden, on the terrace or on the balcony. Animals and birds drink this water during summers when it is hard to find water.
- We should give clean and healthy food to our pets or any other animals living near our house.
- We should keep the animal homes clean.
- We should play with our pets regularly.

We should play with our pet

We should bathe our pets regularly

plough: to dig and turn over a field or other area of land; **thresh:** to separate grain from wheat or other plants; **veterinary doctor:** a doctor who takes care of animals

Animal Homes

Animals, like humans, need a place to live to protect themselves and their young ones from other animals and from heat, rain and cold.

Some animals live in rivers, lakes and seas. A fish can live only in water. Animals like crocodiles and frogs live in both water and on land.

Some animals live in water

Lions and tigers live in caves

Wild animals choose to live in places where they get plenty of food. Some animals live in the forests. Some live under the shade of trees or in caves. Animals like lions, tigers and bears live in caves.

Domestic animals like cows and buffaloes live in **sheds**, horses live in **stables** and hens live in a **coop**. Their homes are man-made.

Coop

Shed

Stable

Some animals live on treetops and in nests

Rabbits live in holes in the ground known as **burrows**. Rats, snakes and ants make **holes** in the ground and live in them.

Rabbits live in burrows and snakes live in holes

Animals like monkeys, squirrels and birds live on **treetops**. Birds live in **nests**.

Pets like dogs live in **kennels**.

Kennel

Wrap up

- Animals are found everywhere—on land, in water. Some can live both on land and in water.
- Wild animals are those animals which live in the forest. They do not like to live around humans.
- Domestic animals are animals which live with humans.
- Animals that are kept in our house are called pet animals.
- Domestic and pet animals live in man-made homes.
- Animals have different types of food.
- Animals move from one place to another in search of food and shelter.
- Animals are useful to us in many ways.

Brush up

A Fill in the blanks with the correct answers.

1. Giraffes are .... animals. (domestic/wild)
2. A dog lives in a .... (kennel/shed)
3. A lion is a .... animal. (grass-eating/flesh-eating)
4. Zebras live in .... (houses/forests)
5. Birds can fly with the help of their .... (feet/wings)

B Tick (✓) the correct sentences and cross (×) the incorrect ones.

1. Cows and horses are domestic animals. ☐
2. All animals eat same kind of food. ☐
3. Different animals move in different ways. ☐
4. Monkeys are used as a means of transport. ☐
5. Animals move from one place to another in search of food and shelter. ☐

C Match the following.

1. Plant-eating animal — a. 

2. Burrow — b. 

3. Milk — c. 

4. Wild animal — d. 

5. Seafood — e. 

D Answer these questions.

1. Where do wild animals live?
2. Define:

   a. Wild animals b. Domestic animals c. Pet animals
3. How do birds and earthworms move?
4. How are animals useful to us? Mention three ways in which they help us.
5. Where do these animals live?

   a. Horses b. Hens c. Cows d. Dogs

Learn the ropes

Domestic animals help us in many ways. They do different kinds of work on fields and even carry loads. What should be done to ensure that these animals do not get hurt or overworked?

Put your heads together

Play an 'animal quiz' in the class. Form two teams—Team A and Team B. Each group can choose an animal and draw or paste its picture on a drawing sheet. A student from Team A can show the picture and a student from Team B has to identify the animal, name its type, its home and the food it eats. Then, a student from Team B can ask the same questions about a different animal to Team A.

Cross connect

Make a paper-plate-bird

You will need one paper plate and two sheets of coloured paper.

1. Fold one sheet of coloured paper like a paper fan. Use this as the wings of the bird.
2. Fold the paper plate in half and ask an adult to make a slit in the plate. Pass the wings through the slit.
3. Cut out a tail and a beak from the other coloured paper, and paste them on the plate. Draw the eyes of the bird.

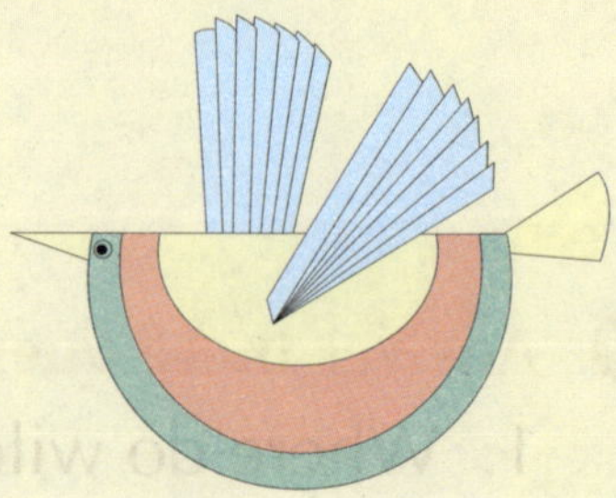

Your paper-plate-bird is ready.

6 People at Work

Get the ball rolling

Have you seen people working in a park? Do any people come to your home to work?

There are many people around us who work to help us and make our life easy. We find such people at work, at home, in school and in our neighbourhood.

Occupations

People do different kinds of work to earn money and make a living. The work done by people for which they get paid is called their **occupation**. People have different occupations. A plumber fixes taps, a farmer grows crops, a greengrocer sells vegetables, a barber cuts hair and a tailor stitches clothes.

Farmer

Plumber

People in Professions

Some people work to take care of our health and safety and to give us knowledge. They are trained for this work. Their work is called a **profession**.

Think through

What do you want to become when you grow up?

A **doctor** treats us when we fall ill so that we can be healthy.

A **nurse** looks after us when we are sick and in hospital.

A **teacher** gives us knowledge and teaches us in school.

Clued in

People in different occupations need special tools to do their work. The tools used by a plumber are different from the tools used by a doctor.

An **engineer** builds roads, bridges, buildings and machines.

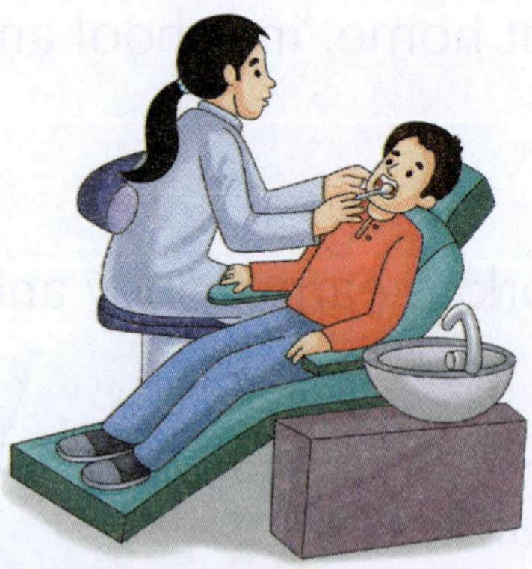

A **dentist** helps us to take care of our teeth and keep them healthy.

A **police officer** makes sure that we are safe.

Give it a shot

Look at the pictures and match the people with the work they do.

1. 

2. 

3. 

4. 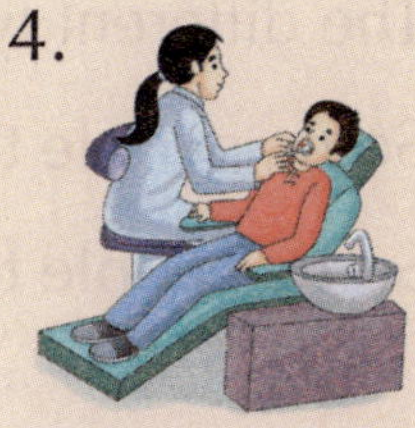

a. Stitches clothes b. Takes care of teeth c. Keeps us safe d. Grows food

People also turn their hobbies into their professions. For example, a person who likes drawing and painting can become an artist.

A **dancer** **performs** on stage.

An **artist** paints different kinds of pictures.

A **singer** sings on stage or in films and music albums.

An **actor** acts in plays, films or in television shows.

A **sportsperson** plays a sport.

A **musician** creates music.

We should respect people who work for us and help make our lives easy. We should be kind to them.

perform: carry out, accomplish, or fulfil (an action, task, or function)

Wrap up

* There are many people who work to help us and to make our lives easy.
* The different types of work people do to earn money are their occupations.
* Some people take training to do their work. Their work is called a profession.
* Some people turn their hobby into their profession.

Brush up

A Who am I?

1. I act in plays and films ....
2. I build roads, buildings and bridges ....
3. I repair broken taps ....
4. I paint different kinds of pictures ....
5. I teach you in school ....

B Name the people using the words given in the box.

Postman	Milkman	Bus driver	Tailor
Carpenter	Barber	Greengrocer	

1. ....
2. ....
3. ....
4. ....
5. ....
6. ....
7. ....

Ⓒ Write T for true and F for false.

1. A musician creates music.
2. A plumber fixes fans and lights.
3. A tailor sells fruits and vegetables.
4. A nurse looks after us when we are sick.
5. We go to a dentist to straighten our teeth.

Ⓓ Answer these questions.

1. What is an occupation?
2. How should we treat people who help us?
3. What work does a greengrocer, a plumber and a nurse do?
4. Name three hobbies that can be taken up as professions.
5. Name any four occupations of people who help us in our daily lives.

Learn the ropes

There are helpers who clean our schools. We can in turn help them by keeping our classroom and school clean. How will you ensure that the trash in your classroom is thrown in the dustbins? What will you do to stop your classmates from throwing garbage on the floor or inside the drawers?

Put your heads together

There are many people who work at our homes and at schools to make our life easier. Besides all these people, our parents also do a lot of things to keep us safe and healthy. In groups, make a list of the things that our parents or helpers do to make life easy for us. Write about things you can do for them as a way of saying thank you.

Cross connect

Name your favourite people in acting, sports, teaching and singing. Find their pictures and paste them in your notebook.

7 Eating Food

Get the ball rolling

Do you eat food which makes you healthy? Talk about it in the class.

All living things need food to live. It keeps us healthy and provides us with energy to work and play. We get food from plants and animals.

Food from Plants and Animals

We get **cereals** and **pulses** from the seeds of some plants. Cereals are also called **food grains**. Rice, wheat and corn are some cereals. Gram and rajma are some pulses.

Wheat

Rajma

Mango, apple, guava and orange are some **fruits** we get from plants. We get **vegetables** such as tomato, brinjal and cauliflower from plants.

Apples

Brinjals

We get **nuts** from plants. Almond, cashew nuts and walnuts are some examples.

Almonds

We get **spices** such as pepper, clove and cardamom from plants. They add **flavour** to our food. **Oil** is obtained from the seeds of some plants. Sunflower and mustard are some examples.

Cloves

Mustard seeds

We get milk, eggs, honey, fish and meat from animals.

Honey

Eggs

Meat

Milk

Fish

Types of Food

There are different kinds of food. They give us energy, build our bodies and protect us from diseases.

Food items that gives us energy are called **energy-giving food**. We need energy to work and play. Rice, potato, sugar, butter and ghee give us energy.

Potato

Sugar

Butter

Rice

Food items that make our bones and muscles strong are called **body-building food**. Soybeans, pulses, eggs, milk and **milk products**, seafood, chicken and fish build our body.

Milk and eggs

Soybean

Fish

Clued in

Milk is the only food that has the qualities of all three kinds of food. Babies should be given milk as it is a complete food.

flavour: how food or drink tastes; **milk products**: food items made from milk such as curd, cheese and butter

Food items that protect us from diseases are called **protective food**. Fruits, vegetables and milk are some examples. All fruits are eaten raw. Most vegetables are cooked and eaten but some vegetables can be eaten raw.

Fruits and vegetables

We should eat food from all the three groups to stay fit and healthy. People who eat eggs, fish and meat are called **non-vegetarians**. People who eat only vegetables, milk and its products are called **vegetarians**.

Water is very important for our body. We should drink 6 to 8 glasses of water every day.

Give it a shot

Write the names of the food items that you eat. Do this for a period of four days in your notebook. List them under three headings—energy-giving food, body-building food and protective food. You can ask an adult to help you.

Good and Healthy Eating Habits

3 GOOD HEALTH AND WELL-BEING

We should follow these healthy eating habits for good health:

- Eat healthy food as it makes the body strong and able to fight diseases.
- Eat our meals on time
- Eat all types of food and drink plenty of water
- Not eat too many sweets or **junk food**
- Eat fresh and well-cooked food
- Chew food slowly and not talk while eating
- Wash our hands before and after eating meals
- Avoid **overeating**
- Avoid eating uncovered food
- Avoid wasting food and water

Think through

Why should we not eat uncovered food?

junk food: food that is not healthy and should be eaten in very less quantities; **overeat:** to eat more than you need

Wrap up

- We all need food to live. Food gives us energy to work and play.
- There are three types of food—energy-giving food, body-building food and protective food.
- We should eat all types of food.
- We should drink plenty of water.
- We should follow good and healthy eating habits.

Brush up

A Circle the odd one out.

1. potato	sugar	apple	chocolate
2. cauliflower	ghee	apple	brinjal
3. paneer	milk	curd	rice
4. coriander	cumin	fish	clove
5. cashew	peanut	green peas	almonds

B Tick (✓) the correct sentences and cross (×) the incorrect ones.

1. All fruits are eaten raw. ☐
2. We should not overeat. ☐
3. We should wash our hands only after eating. ☐
4. We should chew our food fast. ☐
5. We should not waste food. ☐

C Fill in the blanks.

1. Most vegetables are .... and eaten.
2. People who eat eggs, fish and meat are called ....
3. People who eat vegetables, milk and its products are called ....

4. Food items that give us energy are called ....
5. We should drink 6 to 8 glasses of .... every day.

D Answer these questions.

1. What is protective food? Give three examples.
2. What is body-building food? Give three examples.
3. What is energy-giving food? Give three examples.
4. Write any five healthy eating habits.
5. Why should we not eat junk food?

Learn the ropes

Find out how you can use fruit and vegetable peels to help plants in your house grow.

Put your heads together

In groups, draw pictures of food you usually eat for breakfast, lunch and dinner. Write their names and compare the food you eat with that of your group members.

Cross connect

Broccoli Salad

Materials needed: Broccoli, raisins, almonds, 1 cup boiled corn, carrots, creamy cheese, a mixing bowl, salt and pepper.

Ask an elder at your home to chop broccoli and carrots for you. Pack them in a box and add raisins, almonds and boiled corn. Pack some creamy cheese also. Bring it to the class and mix all the items in a bowl. Sprinkle some salt and pepper and your broccoli salad is ready.

8 Water in Our Lives

Get the ball rolling

How can you help to save water? Discuss it in class.

Water is important for all living things. Animals need water to drink and bathe. Plants use water to make their food.

Sources of Water

Rain is the main **source** of water on the Earth. **Rainwater** collects in **puddles**, ponds, lakes, rivers, seas and oceans. These are known as **water bodies**.

Pond

Lake

River

source: a place or a thing from which you get something; **puddles**: a small pool of water that has spread on the ground

Rainwater that collects deep under the ground between rocks, sand and clay is called **groundwater**. **Wells** are dug deep into the ground to get groundwater. A rope is tied to a bucket and water is drawn from the well. Groundwater is also pumped using a **hand pump** or a **tube well**.

Well

Clued in

When it does not rain enough, we need to store a lot of water. Dams are built for this purpose.

Uses of Water

We use water in our daily lives for many things.

We use water for **cooking**.

We use water for **bathing**.

We use water for **washing** and **cleaning**.

We use water to help plants grow.

Water is used for making electricity.

Water is used to put out fires.

Can you think of more uses of water?

....

....

Storing Water

We need to store water to keep it for later use. Stored water can be used for drinking, cooking and washing. Drinking water can be stored in jugs, earthen pots and bottles. Water for bathing and washing is stored in plastic buckets, steel buckets, drums and tanks.

Bucket

Bottle

Earthen pot

Give it a shot

Write names or draw pictures of objects in which you store water at home. What are the sources of water in your city, town or village?

Drinking Water

Drinking water is the water which is clean and safe for drinking. It is also used for cooking food. Water from the tap is not fit for drinking. It has to be boiled or **filtered** before drinking. Boiling kills the germs present in water. We should store drinking water in covered containers.

Saving Water

We should not waste water. We can start this by saving water at homes.

- We should close the tap while and after brushing the teeth.
- Water should not be wasted while bathing.
- All leaking taps and pipes should be **repaired**.
- We can collect rainwater in underground tanks.

Collecting rainwater

Keeping Water Clean

We must keep water clean. Water which contains **germs** makes us sick.

- People should not bathe or wash clothes in rivers or ponds.

Think through

How can we use rainwater?

filtered: passing water through an object that cleans it; **repaired**: to mend something that is damaged or is not working; **germs**: a very small living thing that we cannot see and which makes us sick

- Waste or garbage should not be thrown into water bodies.
- Waste water should not be allowed to drain into rivers or lakes.
- We should explain the importance of keeping water clean to our family and friends.

Wrap up

- All living things need water to live.
- We store water to keep it for later use.
- Water from the tap is not fit for drinking.
- Water is boiled and filtered to kill germs present in it.
- We should save water.
- All water bodies should be kept clean.

Brush up

A Circle the odd one out.

1. jug	glass	bottle	puddle
2. river	lakes	well	pond
3. jump	drink	wash	cook
4. tank	sea	drum	bucket

B Fill in the blanks.

1. Water can be used for ...., ... and ....
2. Rainwater collects deep under the ground between rocks, ... and clay.
3. Lakes, ponds, rivers and seas are known as ....
4. Groundwater is pumped out by using hand pump or ....
5. Tap water should be .... or .... before drinking.

C Match the following.

1.	Water bodies	a.	Closing taps after use
2.	Storing water	b.	Bathing
3.	Save water	c.	Well
4.	Uses of water	d.	Earthen pots
5.	Ground water	e.	Rivers

D Answer these questions.

1. Name five sources of water.
2. Where does rainwater collect?
3. What are the uses of water?
4. Write three ways in which water can be saved.
5. Write two ways of keeping water clean.

Learn the ropes

How do you think throwing waste materials in water bodies affects the fish, plants and other animals living in them?

Put your heads together

In groups, make a list of activities that we do at home using water. Compare your lists with the other groups and find out which activities require water the most. How will you try to use less water every day?

Cross connect

Bottle watering can

Materials required: an old plastic bottle, a thick pin to make holes

1. Take an old plastic bottle and clean it.
2. With the help of an adult, punch holes in the cap of the bottle. Make sure the holes are big enough to let the water flow.
3. Fill the bottle with water and fasten the cap. Your bottle watering can is ready!

9 Air Around Us

Get the ball rolling

Look at this picture. Talk about it in class.

Air is all around us. We cannot see air. We can only feel it when it moves. All living things need air to breathe.

Moving air is called **wind**. It makes the clouds move and the kites fly. Air that blows gently is called **breeze**. When wind moves very fast, it is called a **storm**.

Breeze

Wind

Storm

Properties of Air

Air has **weight** but does not have any shape.

Air takes up **space**. When we blow air into a balloon, it fills the space inside the balloon.

Air moves in a **direction**. The direction in which trees and grass bend is the direction of the wind.

Moving air has **force**. Storms can **uproot** plants and cause damage to buildings, animals and human beings.

Clued in

A very strong wind is called a gale.

Give it a shot

A. Take a balloon and blow air into it with the help of an elder. What happens to the balloon? The balloon becomes big. This is because **air takes up space** inside the balloon.

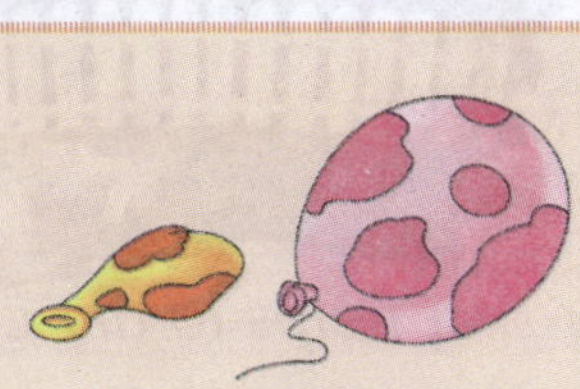

B. Take two balloons. Blow air into one of the balloons and tie it to one end of a hanger. Tie the second balloon to the other end of the hanger without blowing air into it. What do you see? The hanger tilts towards the balloon filled with air. This is because **air has weight**.

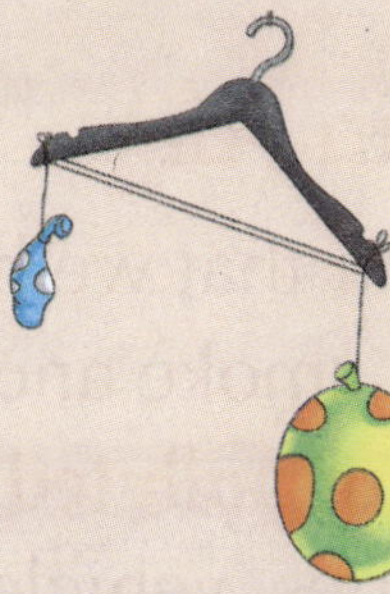

Uses of Air

Air is very important for us and has many uses.

- A gas called oxygen, present in the air, helps us breathe.
- Plants use a gas called carbon dioxide present in the air to make their own food.
- Oxygen, present in the air, helps us make fire.
- We can hear sound only because there is air around us.
- Electricity is produced from moving wind.
- Air also moves the blades of **windmills**.

Windmill

uproot: to pull something out of the ground; **windmills**: buildings with long pieces of wood on the outside which turn around as the wind blows

- We **inflate** balloons and tyres of vehicles with air.
- Wind makes the clothes dry faster.
- Birds and aeroplanes fly in the air.
- Hot air makes air balloons rise.
- Sailboats and gliders move because of wind.

Aeroplane flies in air

Air helps to dry clothes

Air helps balloons to rise

Air moves sailboats

Clean Air

The air that we breathe should be clean. Dust, smoke and germs make the air dirty or **polluted**. Harmful gases from factories, vehicles and burning wood make the air dirty. Polluted air is not good for us. We can become sick or have a bad cough due to polluted air. We should plant more trees as they make the air clean.

Think through

Why does the air smell bad sometimes?

Wrap up

- Air is all around us.
- We breathe in oxygen from the air.
- Air does not have any shape. It occupies space and it has weight.
- We need clean and fresh air to breathe.
- Dust, smoke and germs make the air dirty.
- Trees make the air clean.
- Air has many uses for us.

inflate: to become bigger when filled with air or a gas

Brush up

A Fill in the blanks with the correct answers.

1. When air blows gently, it is called .... (storm/breeze)
2. When wind moves fast, it is called .... (breeze/storm)
3. Air has .... and takes up space. (height/weight)
4. Plants use .... present in air to make their own food. (oxygen/carbon dioxide)
5. .... can be produced from moving wind. (Electricity/Oxygen)

B Tick (✓) the correct sentences and cross (×) the incorrect ones.

1. We hear sound only because there is air around us. ☐
2. We need clean and fresh air to breathe. ☐
3. Birds and aeroplanes fly in the air. ☐
4. We can see air. ☐

C Fill in the blanks.

1. A .... can cause damage to buildings and human beings.
2. .... present in air helps us to make fire.
3. Dust and smoke make the air ....
4. .... more trees to make the air clean.

D Answer these questions.

1. What is a breeze?
2. What is wind?
3. What is a storm?
4. Write four uses of air.
5. Why should we plant trees?

Learn the ropes

Tick (✓) the things that can be done to keep the air clean.

1. Burn leaves and crackers
2. Plant trees
3. Walk for short distances
4. Sneeze and cough without covering the mouth

Put your heads together

In groups of four, make a poster about uses of air. You can decorate your poster by making drawings and colouring them.

Cross connect

Make a paper decoration

Materials needed: 4 sheets of different coloured paper, strings, a pair of scissors, glue

1. Take a sheet of coloured paper. Fold it in half and with the help of an elder, cut small triangles.
2. Open out the triangles such that they are joined at the fold.
3. Cut out triangles in different colours.
4. Take a string and place open triangles on it.
5. Glue the pieces of paper with the string inside.
6. Your paper decoration is ready.

10 School is Fun

Get the ball rolling

Have you gone on a school picnic? What are some of the fun things you do in school?

A school is a place where we study and learn new things. We learn to read, write, count, work and make friends in school. We also get to know our **classmates** in school.

Things We Learn in School

We learn many things in school.

Reading and writing

Using computers

Singing and dancing

Painting, drawing and art

Playing sports

Clued in

Many years ago, teachers were called **gurus** and schools were called **gurukuls**.

People in School

Many people in a school help us so that we can learn, have fun and feel safe.

Principal

The **Principal** is the head of the school. She or he takes care of everything in the school.

Different **teachers** teach us different subjects. They all teach us good manners. They also teach us how to behave with each other in the class. We must obey and respect our teachers.

The **peon** rings the bell to let us know that the class is over. He also helps the Principal and the teachers with their work.

Guard

The school **guard** is always at the gate of the school. He keeps us safe by checking who enters or leaves the school building.

Cleaners

Cleaners sweep and **mop** to clean the school every day. They clean in the morning before we reach and in the afternoon after we leave school. We can help them by keeping our classroom neat and clean and by throwing the **trash** in the dustbin.

We must respect all the people who work in the school and take care of us.

mop: a tool for washing floors that has a long handle; **trash**: things that you throw away because you no longer want or need them

Places in School

A **computer lab** is a place where the computers are kept. A **lab assistant** looks after the computers and helps us if anything goes wrong with them. A computer teacher teaches us how to use the computers.

A **library** is a place where many books are kept. The teacher in the library, also called **librarian**, helps us find books to read. He or she also keeps the library neat and sometimes even reads stories to us.

Library

Playing area

There is also a **playing area** or an **activity room** in the school where we can play different games and have fun with our friends. In the playing area, we play different sports like cricket and football.

Give it a shot

It is said that the years we spend in school are the most fun times of our lives. Find out the following information about the school that you go to.

- The motto of your school ....
- The name of your school Principal ....
- The name of the first Principal of your school ....
- The year your school was started ....

Fun in School

Special days like Teacher's Day, Children's Day, school picnic, annual day and sports day are times of great fun as we learn to work and celebrate together. Teacher's Day is celebrated on 5 September and Children's Day is celebrated on 14 November. We also celebrate different festivals in school. We learn about them in school assemblies while celebrating these special days.

Think through

Why is Teacher's Day celebrated only on 5 September and not on any other day? What is special about this day?

Respect for School

We must respect our school by taking care of the places and the things we use in the school. We should also respect the people in our school. We must take care of our classmates.

We should put things back after using them.

We should not write on the library books or tear their pages.

We should throw trash in the dustbin.

We should not pluck flowers or break the plants growing in the school.

We should not **scribble** on walls, desks and chairs in the classroom.

We should wait for our turn while playing in the playground.

We should clean the blackboard and **arrange** the chairs in our classroom to keep it clean.

We should decorate our classroom.

We should respect our teachers.

scribble: to write something quickly; **arrange**: to plan or organize something

Wrap up

- We study, play, make friends and have fun in school.
- The teachers in the school teach us many things.
- The Principal is the head of the school.
- A school has many special places where we learn and play.
- Special days and festivals are celebrated in schools.
- We must respect all the people in the school and keep our school neat and clean.

Brush up

A Draw a ☺ for the true sentences and a ☹ for the false ones.

1. We can throw paper and food in our classroom.
2. A school is a place where we can only study.
3. The Principal is the head of the school.
4. We should pluck the flowers in a school.
5. Teachers only play games with us.

B Fill in the blanks.

1. We get many books to read in the ....
2. A .... helps us to know that a period is over.
3. The .... is the head of a school.
4. .... sweep and mop the school every day.
5. .... is a festival celebrated in school.

C Match the following.

1. Teacher's Day	a. Lab Assistant
2. Children's Day	b. Librarian
3. Computer lab	c. 14 November
4. Library	d. Teacher
5. Classroom	e. 5 September

D **Answer these questions.**

1. Name any four things that you learn in a school.
2. Who is a librarian and what does he or she do?
3. What does a peon in a school do?
4. What do we do in the computer lab?
5. Name some of the special days celebrated in your school.

Learn the ropes

Find out the names of all the people in your school who help you. Talk about the way they help you in class.

1. The peon who sits outside the Principal's office ....
2. The school guard ....
3. The school librarian ....
4. The computer teacher ....

Put your heads together

One way in which we can show respect for our school is by keeping our classroom clean and throwing the trash in the dustbins. In groups, make three different dustbins for your classroom to make it easy to collect waste. You can make a blue bin for paper, a green bin for food and fruit skins and a red bin for plastic wrappers, tin, foil and plastic bottles.

Cross connect

Celebrate School's Birthday

Find out when your school was founded. This is the birthday of your school. Plan a class assembly to celebrate your school's birthday. You can make invitation cards for the teachers and the Principal requesting them to attend the celebration.

11 Houses People Live In

Get the ball rolling

What kind of house do you live in? Have you seen a building that has many houses in it?

A house protects us from heat, rain, storms and cold. During hot summers, a house keeps us cool and away from the hot sun. During cold winters, a house keeps us warm. It also protects us from thieves, wild animals and insects.

Types of Houses

Houses are made differently in different places. There are three main types of houses—**kutcha houses**, **pucca houses** and **temporary houses**.

A kutcha house

Kutcha houses

We have learnt that most people in the villages live in **huts**. The roofs of huts are made of straw, leaves and bamboo. They are constructed with mud, straw, leaves and wood, which are easily available in the villages and are not **expensive**. These kinds of houses are called kutcha because they are not very strong. They can break during storms or flow away in floods.

Pucca houses

Pucca houses are strong houses made of brick, cement, steel and stone. Pucca houses are permanent houses as they cannot be **destroyed** easily by wind or water.

Pucca houses can be **single-storey** houses, **double-storey** houses or **bungalows**. They can also be **apartments** in very tall buildings called **multi-storey buildings**.

Clued in

Houses in places where it snows or rains have sloping roofs to allow snow to slide off easily. This prevents water from collecting on the roof. Houses built in warmer places have flat roofs.

A single-storey pucca house

A double-storey house has two floors

A bungalow is a large house

Apartments or flats are houses in a multi-storey buildings

Temporary houses

Temporary houses, such as a **tent** and a **caravan** can be moved from one place to another. Tents can even be carried in a bag. They are made of **canvas** and can be easily fixed to the ground. Tents are mostly used for **camping**.

A caravan is a small house attached to a car or a van. The whole house can be driven from one place to another. They are also known as houses on wheels.

A caravan and a tent

expensive: costing a lot of money; **destroyed**: to damage something so badly that it no longer works or exists; **canvas**: a strong, rough material used for making tents; **camping**: living in a tent

Special Houses

There are also some special houses. These are not found everywhere, but only in certain places.

Stilt house

Stilt houses are built on legs made of bamboo called **stilts**. These houses are made in places where it rains heavily.

Igloos are houses made of snow. These are made in places where it is cold and it snows throughout the year.

Houseboats are houses built on boats. They **float** on water.

Igloo

Houseboat

Give it a shot

Look at the pictures and name the type of houses.

1. .... 2. .... 3. ....

Parts of a House

A house has many rooms with doors and windows. There is a roof on top of a house. The walls inside the house separate one room from another. The rooms have different names like bedroom, dining room, sitting room and kitchen. Houses have a main door in front for **entrance**.

Parts of a house

stilts: straight poles that support a building so that it is high above the ground or water; **float:** to move slowly on water

Clean Home

We can keep our home clean in the following ways:

- All rooms of the house should be dusted, swept and mopped regularly.
- The kitchen and the bathrooms should be kept dry.
- Trash should be thrown in dustbins covered with **lid**s to keep mosquitoes and flies away.
- Books, clothes and toys should be put away in their proper places.
- Windows should be left open to let **ample** sunlight and fresh air come in. Sunlight helps kill germs.
- Windows should be covered with wire netting to keep insects out.

Think through

Name some people who help us build houses.

Wrap up

* We all need a house to live in.
* A house keeps us safe and protects us from the weather, thieves and wild animals.
* There are different kinds of houses: kutcha houses, pucca houses and temporary houses.
* There are also some special houses. These are not found everywhere, but only in certain places.
* A house has many rooms separated by walls inside the house.
* We should keep our house neat and clean to stay healthy.

Brush up

A **Choose the correct answers.**

1. A moving house is also called a

   a. kutcha house　　b. pucca house

   c. temporary house　　d. permanent house

lid: a cover; **ample**: enough

2. A tent is made of

a. cement b. bamboo c. ice d. canvas

3. These houses are built on legs made of bamboo

a. stilt houses b. huts c. igloos d. bungalows

4. These are needed in a house for the people to stay healthy

a. sunlight b. fresh air c. wire netting d. all of these

5. A house keeps us safe from

a. rain b. storm c. thieves d. all of these

B Fill in the blanks.

1. A .... is a house on wheels.
2. .... are houses found in very cold places.
3. Houses that float on water are called ....
4. Most people in the villages live in .... houses.
5. People who live in .... can carry their houses in a bag.

C Match the following.

1.  a. Temporary house

2.  b. Kutcha house

3.  c. Double-storey house

4.  d. Apartment building

D Answer these questions.

1. What is the difference between a kutcha and a pucca house?
2. Name the parts of a house.
3. Why should the windows in a house have wire netting on them?

Learn the ropes

It is important to keep our houses clean. Make a list of the things you do to keep your house clean.

Put your heads together

Form groups of three and make a cut-out of a house from coloured paper. One student can draw the outline of the house, one can take charge of cutting the paper with the help of the teacher and one can paste the cut-out on a chart paper. You can also make a paper chain family to go with your house. You can also add things like a car or some plants and trees.

Cross connect

An Old Woman Who Lived in the Shoe

Read out this poem in class.

There was an old woman who lived in a shoe.

She had so many children, she did not know what to do;

She gave them some soup without any bread,

She hugged them all happily and put them to bed.

In groups, try to write a poem about a house. Here are the opening lines:

Quiet now, do not make a sound

We have reached Grandma's house...

12 Our Surroundings

Get the ball rolling

Are there any shops in your neighbourhood? Name some of the places in your neighbourhood.

Look around your house. What do you see? You will find many houses and places such as a market or a park. This area around our house makes up our **neighbourhood**. The families or people who live near our house are our **neighbours**.

Some neighbourhoods have places like a market, a park, a post office, a hospital or a doctor's clinic, a bus stop, a school, a police station, a bank and places of worship. These are called **neighbourhood services**. Such neighbourhoods are well-developed.

Places in a Neighbourhood

A **market** has many shops that sell different things. A person who sells things in a shop is called a **shopkeeper**. People can buy things of daily needs from the neighbourhood market.

A **park** is a place of **recreation**. People go to the park to relax and enjoy. People of all ages walk, do yoga, exercise or jog in the park. The children have fun on the swings or play games.

A park

> **Clued in**
>
> Many grocery shops these days have been replaced by huge departmental stores. Groceries can also be bought online.

Some neighbourhoods have **schools**. Children go to school to learn and study. They also play games and make friends in a school.

A school

A bus stop

Do you go to school by bus? Then you must be going to the **bus stop** in your neighbourhood every morning to **board** it. A bus stop is a place where we wait to board a bus.

Many neighbourhoods have a **clinic** or a **hospital**. We see a doctor at his or her clinic or go to a hospital when we are sick. A doctor **examines** us and gives us medicines to get well.

A hospital

Hospitals have **ambulances** that bring sick and injured people to the hospital during an **emergency** so that they can be given immediate care. To call an ambulance, we should dial 102.

recreation: an activity done for fun; **board**: to get in; **examine**: to study something very carefully; **emergency**: something that happens suddenly and needs immediate action

Some neighbourhoods have banks. A **bank** is a safe place to keep our money and other **valuables**. A bank manager looks after the bank.

Bank

A police station

A **police station** is a place where police officers work. Police officers protect us by keeping our neighbourhood safe from danger. To get help from the police, we should call 100.

A fire station

In case of a fire in our neighbourhood, we must immediately call the fire station. A **fire station** has red coloured vans called **fire engines**. The people who come in these vans to put out the fire and **rescue** us are **firefighters**. They use water, ladders and pipes to put out the fires. In case of a fire emergency, we should call 101 and ask the fire station to send their **fire brigade**.

Neighbourhoods also have different **places of worship** such as temple, gurdwara, mosque or a church where people can pray.

A post office

A **post office** in the neighbourhood is a place where we go to buy stamps and postcards. We send postcards, letters and parcels to our friends, family members or to people for work.

Give it a shot

Aarav has written a letter to his school Principal and has put it in an envelope. Where should Aarav paste the stamp—the box on the left or the box on the right? Write the word 'stamp' in the correct box. Then, write your school address in the space given below the stamps.

valuables: costly things; **rescue:** to save somebody from a harmful situation

Good Neighbours

Good neighbours share their joys and sorrows and help one another in times of need. We too can be good to our neighbours by being friendly, helpful and keeping our neighbourhood clean.

Think through

Aarav saw fire coming out of his neighbour's house. He quickly picked up the phone and called his father who was in office. What else could Aarav have done? Who should he have called?

Wrap up

* The houses and the area around our house is our neighbourhood.
* The families who live in houses near us are our neighbours.
* A neighbourhood has many places like a market, bus stop, school, hospital, park, post office and a bank.
* There are different places of worship in a neighbourhood.
* Good neighbours share their joys and sorrows and help in times of need.

Brush up

A Match the following.

1. Daily needs	a. Post office
2. Recreation	b. Market
3. Ambulance	c. Fire station
4. Fire engine	d. Park
5. Postcards	e. Hospital

B Fill in the blanks with the correct answers.

1. A .... looks after our money. (police station/bank)
2. We go to a .... for recreation. (school/park)
3. We go to a .... to send a parcel. (post office/fire station)
4. We are sent to a .... when we are very sick. (church/hospital)
5. We go to a .... to buy soaps and toothpaste. (shopkeeper/greengrocer)

C **Draw a 🙂 for the true sentences and a ☹ for the false ones.**

1. The families that live in houses near our houses are our neighbours.
2. Ambulances are sent only during an emergency.
3. We will go to a hospital for help if our money has been stolen.
4. We dial 100 to call a fire station.
5. We go to school to learn to read and write.

D **Answer these questions.**

1. When is a neighbourhood called well-developed?
2. What can we buy from a post office?
3. How does a fire station help us?
4. How is a park a place of recreation for people of all ages?
5. How can we be good neighbours?

Learn the ropes

Make a list of all the services in your neighbourhood. Find out the phone numbers of some of the important places such as chemist, greengrocer, hospital, bank and the water and electricity supply office. Make a list of these numbers and stick it on the fridge.

Put your heads together

Visit a market in your neighbourhood with your parents. Is the market dirty and littered or is it clean? Write your observations in your notebook. The next day, discuss in groups in your classroom the ways to keep the neighbourhood markets clean.

Cross connect

How do you imagine a good neighbourhood to be? In your notebook, draw and colour it.

13 Our Earth

Get the ball rolling

Have you seen a mountain or a river or sea? Talk about them in class.

The Earth is our home. It is round like an orange and moves around the Sun. It is made up of land and water.

The Earth

A globe

Three parts of the Earth are covered with water and one part is made up of land. The Earth is also known as the **blue planet** because it has more water than land. A sphere-shaped model of the Earth is called a **globe**.

Clued in

The shape of the Earth is a sphere which is slightly flattened at the top and the bottom.

Landforms

Land is not the same everywhere. There are hills, mountains, valleys, deserts, plains and islands on the Earth. These natural features of the Earth are called **landforms**.

A **hill** is a landform that is higher than the land surrounding it. Hills look like cones.

A **mountain** is a landform that rises high above its surroundings. It is taller than a hill. A mountain usually has **steep** slopes and rounded or sharp peaks. Some mountains are covered with snow.

A **valley** is a low area of land, lying between two higher parts of land that might be hills or mountains.

A **plain** is a flat area of land. Plains occur as lowlands at the base of valleys and mountains. People grow crops and fruits in plains.

Hills and mountains

A valley

A plain

A **desert** is a large region that receives very little rain each year. It is covered with sand and rocks. Very few plants like cactus and animals like camel live in deserts.

An **island** is an area of land that is surrounded by water. Islands are found in most water bodies.

A **forest** is an area of land where many trees grow. Many animals live in forests. Forests are very important and grow in many places around the world.

A desert

An island

A forest

steep: rising at a sharp angle

Water on the Earth

We have already learnt that a large part of the Earth's surface is covered with water. The water on the Earth is found in different types of water bodies.

A **river** is a flowing stream of water. Water in a river comes either from rain or from the melting snow of the mountains. The water in a river is freshwater. A river flows towards the sea and most of the rivers meet the sea.

A large body of water surrounded by land is known as a **lake**. It contains freshwater. Lakes are fairly still bodies of water as compared to a river, in which the water keeps on flowing.

> **Think through**
>
> Why is seawater salty?

A **sea** is a large body of water. Seawater is salty.

Oceans are water bodies that are bigger than seas. Ocean water is salty too.

A river

A lake

A sea

Give it a shot

India has different types of landforms and water bodies. Name one of each.

1. Mountain ....
2. River ....
3. Hill ....
4. Plain ....
5. Island ....
6. Desert ....
7. Sea ....
8. Forest/Lake ....

13 CLIMATE ACTION

Clean and Green Earth

The Earth provides us with land to live, air to breathe, water to drink and food to eat. We must take care of it. We should keep it clean and plant more trees. We must keep all water bodies clean and save water.

Wrap up

- The Earth is made of land and water.
- Some of the landforms on the Earth are hills, mountains, valleys, plains, islands, deserts and forests.
- Rivers lakes, seas and oceans are the different types of water bodies on the Earth.
- We should try to keep the Earth and its water bodies clean.

Brush up

A **Unscramble these words to get the names of different landforms.**

1. SINDAL ....
2. SEFTOR ....
3. NONUMAIT ....
4. LAYVEL ....
5. TEDSER ....

B **Fill in the blanks with the correct answers.**

1. The Earth is also known as the .... planet. (red/blue)
2. A sphere-shaped model of the Earth is called a .... (ball/globe)
3. A .... is a low area of land lying between two higher parts of land which might be hills or mountains. (valley/desert)
4. A .... is a large region that gets very little rain each year. (desert/forest)
5. A .... is a flowing stream of water. (river/lake)

C **Draw a ☺ for the correct sentences and ☹ for the wrong ones.**

1. Mountains are covered with rocks and snow.
2. A sea is a large body of water where rivers meet.
3. A forest is a piece of land with many trees.

4. A valley is a landform that rises high above its surroundings.

5. Oceans are water bodies larger than seas.

D Answer these questions.

1. Why is the Earth known as the blue planet?
2. What is a globe?
3. Name the different landforms. Describe any two of them.
4. What is the difference between river and lake?
5. Why should we keep the Earth clean and green?

Learn the ropes

Look at a map of India and locate one mountain, one desert and two rivers. In your notebook write the names of states in which the mountain and the desert are located. Write the names of the states through which the rivers flow. Take the help of your teacher to read the map.

Put your heads together

Form five groups in class. Each group can take a chart paper and make different landforms and water bodies on it. The materials that you can use to make them are paint, sand, paper, straw, grass and strips of a cloth. Present your chart in class.

Cross connect

Imagine that you are on a trip in India. Write two sentences about at least five landforms and water bodies you visited.

14 Our Universe

Get the ball rolling

Look at this picture. Talk about it in class.

Every morning when we wake up and look at the sky, we see the Sun shining. At night, the same sky turns dark and we see the moon and thousands of stars **twinkling** in the sky. The Sun, the moon, the stars and the Earth are a part of the **universe**.

Day

Night

The Solar System

The Sun, the moon and the Earth belong to a huge family called the **solar system**. There are eight **planets** in the solar system.

Clued in

The solar system once had nine planets. Pluto, the ninth planet, is now a dwarf planet.

twinkling: shining with a light that keeps changing from bright to less bright

They are **Mercury**, **Venus**, **Earth**, **Mars**, **Jupiter**, **Saturn**, **Uranus** and **Neptune**. Each planet moves around the Sun in a fixed path called an **orbit**.

The solar system

The Earth

The Earth is the third planet from the Sun. It is the only planet which has life on it. It spins and moves around the Sun.

The Earth

The Sun

The Sun is a huge ball of fire. It is the nearest star to the Earth. It gives us heat and light. All living things need sunlight. We see the Sun rising in the **east** and setting in the **west** every day.

The Sun

Think through

What would happen if there was no sunlight?

The Moon

The moon moves around the Earth. It is closest to the Earth. The moon is much smaller than the Earth. It is made up of rocks and does not have air around it. It does not have light of its own and gets its light from the Sun. The shape of the moon changes every night. When the moon is round and big like a ball, it is called a **full moon**. When we see no moon in the sky, it is called **new moon**.

New moon

Full moon

Stars

We have seen stars at night in the sky. Stars are very big in size but they appear small as they are far away from us. They have light of their own. They cannot be seen in the daytime as the Sun shines brightly. The Sun is also a star.

Stars in the night sky

Give it a shot

Observe the shape of the moon on the given days of a month and draw each shape you see in the space given below. Does the shape of the moon change often?

My Observations				
Day 1	Day 10	Day 14	Day 20	Day 28

Wrap up

- The Sun, the moon, the stars and the Earth are a part of the universe.
- There are eight planets in the solar system. They are Mercury, Venus, Earth, Mars, Jupiter, Saturn, Uranus and Neptune.
- The Sun is a huge ball of fire. It gives us light and heat.
- Stars are very big in size. They appear small as they are far away from us.
- The Earth is the third planet from the Sun. It is the only planet which has life on it.

Brush up

A **Find 10 words related to the universe from the word grid.**

R	V	E	N	U	S	O	M	E
P	L	A	E	T	A	I	A	M
O	J	U	P	I	T	E	R	E
S	U	N	T	N	U	S	S	R
T	I	N	U	D	R	R	E	C
M	O	O	N	I	N	A	A	U
P	L	U	E	A	R	T	H	R
I	U	R	A	N	U	S	K	Y

B **Fill in the blanks with the correct answers.**

1. The moon gets its light from the .... (Sun/Earth)
2. The Earth is the .... planet from the Sun. (third/fifth)
3. There are .... planets in the solar system. (eight/nine)
4. The shape of the .... changes every night. (Sun/moon)
5. The Earth spins and moves around the .... (Sun/moon)

C **Fill in the blanks.**

1. The Sun, the moon, the stars and the Earth are a part of the ....
2. .... is much smaller than the Earth.
3. .... does not have light of its own. It gets its light from the Sun.
4. We get .... and .... from the Sun.
5. We cannot see the .... in the sky during the day as the .... shines brightly.

D **Answer these questions.**

1. How is the morning sky different from the night sky?
2. How many planets are there in the solar system? Name them.
3. Describe the Sun.
4. What is a full moon and a new moon?
5. Why do stars appear small?

Learn the ropes

The Earth is a beautiful place and we should take care of it. It provides us air and water. Therefore, it is our duty to keep it clean. In five points, explain what you would do to keep the Earth clean.

Put your heads together

In groups, enact the Sun, the moon and the Earth. One student can be the Sun and the rest can walk around it like the planets. Other students can be the Earth and the moon. The Earth will spin and move around the Sun and the moon will move around the Earth.

Cross connect

Shadow Painting

Things needed: A sheet of white drawing paper, small objects like animal figures, a plate, pencil and paint box

Keep an object in a sunny spot and observe where the shadow falls. Place the white paper where the shadow falls. You will observe that the shadow now forms on the white paper. Using a pencil, draw an outline of the shadow carefully on the paper. Paint the outline and add details and a background. Your shadow painting is ready.

15 Seasons and Weather

Get the ball rolling

What do you do when you feel hot while playing? What do you do when it rains?

Weather changes every day. It can be cold, sunny, foggy, rainy, cloudy or windy. Weather can also change many times in a day. It is the day-to-day condition of the air of a particular place.

Rainy

Sunny

Windy

Cold

Seasons

Sometimes the weather stays the same for a long period. This is called a **season**. A season can last for two or three months. Some seasons are hot and some are cold. India has five main seasons. They are **spring**, **summer**, **monsoon**, **autumn** and **winter**. In India, summers are long and winters are short.

Think through

Why do you think change of seasons is important?

Spring is the most colourful season of the year. Flowers bloom and new leaves begin to grow on the trees. The weather is very **pleasant**. Spring lasts from late February till the end of March in India.

Spring

Summer is the hottest season. The Sun is bright and hot. Days are longer than the nights. We wear light cotton clothes. We **sweat** a lot and feel thirsty too. We eat a lot of fruits such as mangoes and melons in the summer. April, May and June are the summer months of India.

Monsoon is a season of heavy rainfall. We hear **thunder** and see **lightning** in the sky in this season. We use umbrellas and raincoats to protect ourselves from heavy rain. July, August and September are the monsoon months. It is also known as the **rainy** season.

Summer

Autumn

Monsoon

During **autumn**, trees shed their leaves. The sky is usually cloudless. It is neither too hot nor too cold during this season. October and November are the autumn months in India.

Clued in

After rain, we sometimes see a **rainbow** in the sky. A rainbow is made up of seven colours.

pleasant: nice, enjoyable, or attractive; **sweat**: liquid which comes out through our skin when we are hot; **thunder**: loud noise that you hear from the sky especially during a storm; **lightning**: very bright flashes of light in the sky

Winter is the coldest season of the year. The days are shorter, and the nights are longer in this season. It rains in some parts of India and snows in the mountainous regions. We wear woollen clothes. We use blankets and quilts to keep ourselves warm. India experiences winter in December, January and early February.

Winter

Give it a shot

Which is your favourite season? Write two things you love about that season. What clothes do you wear? Draw a picture in your notebook showing that season and colour it.

Wrap up

- Weather keeps changing from day to day.
- Spring, summer, monsoon, autumn and winter are the five main seasons of India.
- Spring is a colourful and pleasant season.
- Summer is the hottest season.
- Monsoon is a season of heavy rainfall.
- Trees shed their leaves during autumn.
- Winter is the coldest season.

Brush up

A Fill in the blanks with the correct answers.

1. When the weather stays same for a long time it is called .... (season/monsoon)

2. .... is the most colourful season of the year. (Spring/Autumn)

3. The days are shorter and the nights are longer in .... (winter/summer)

4. Rainy season is also known as .... (autumn/monsoon)

B Match the following.

1.  a. Summer

2.  b. Winter

3.  c. Autumn

4.  d. Spring

5.  e. Monsoon

C Tick (✓) the correct sentences and a cross (×) the incorrect ones.

1. In autumn, it is neither too hot nor too cold.
2. A rainbow is made up of seven colours.
3. The sky is usually cloudless in summer.
4. Light and cotton clothes are worn in summer.
5. Weather changes every day.

D Answer these questions.

1. What is weather?
2. What is season?
3. Write one line each about summer and monsoon.
4. In which season do trees shed their leaves? Write a few lines about this season.
5. What kind of clothes do we wear in winter?

Learn the ropes

Make a weather diary. Note the kind of weather you experience every day for a week. See how quickly the weather changes every day.

Put your heads together

Collect pictures of clothes worn in different seasons and bring them to school. Form five groups. Each group can select one season. One person from each group can show the pictures of clothes to others. The group that correctly names the season in which the clothes are worn, scores a point. Continue playing until you show all the clothes you have got.

Cross connect

Leaf printing

Collect some fallen leaves. Using poster colours paint each leaf on one side. While the paint is still wet, press the leaves on a chart paper. You can use as many leaves as you want. Carefully remove the leaves and let the chart paper dry. Your beautiful leaf painting is ready. You can also make gift wrapping sheets in the same way.

16 Travel and Communicate

Get the ball rolling

Have you seen the vehicles that move on water? Are they different from the ones that move on land?

People travel to visit different places. They go to offices and schools. Some people travel to visit their friends and relatives. Some travel for a holiday.

Thousands of years ago, people would walk from one place to another. It took them very long to travel. Travelling to far off places was very difficult. Later, they learnt to ride animals. They also carried things on those animals. After the wheel was **invented**, travelling became easier. People could reach far off places quickly.

People travelled by riding animals

invented: to think of or make something for the first time

We use different types of vehicles to travel. These vehicles move on land, on water and in the air. Some vehicles have engines and need **fuel** to move. Petrol, diesel and CNG are some fuels. Such vehicles move faster than the vehicles that do not have engines.

The vehicles used for taking people, animals and **goods** from one place to another are called the **means of transport**. They are of three types—land transport, water transport and air transport.

Land Transport

Vehicles that move on land, roads and **tracks** are means of **land transport**. These vehicles need an engine to move. Some land transport vehicles like bullock cart and cycle do not have engines. They do not need fuel and do not make the air dirty. We should try to use them more often. We should walk or cycle to nearby places. This saves fuel.

Car

Auto rickshaw

Scooter

Cycle

Cycle rickshaw

Motorcycle

Bus

Bullock cart

Truck

Trains

A train moves on **tracks** that are laid on land. A train has an engine and many **coaches** in which people sit. We travel by train to go to places that are far from our city or village. Trains take us to different places that are in different parts of the country. They carry people and goods. People on the train are called **passengers**. Trains that carry people are called **passenger trains**. The trains that carry only goods are called **goods trains**. **Metros** are trains that move on tracks inside the same city. They also move underground.

fuel: any material that produces heat or power when it is burnt; **goods**: things that are made to be sold; **tracks:** rails that a train moves along

Passenger train

Goods train

Metro

Water Transport

We can cross rivers, lakes, oceans and seas using **water transport**. Ships, boats, steamers, motorboats and ferries are means of water transport. They are used for transporting both people and goods.

Ship

Sailboat

Ferry

Motorboat

Steamer

Air Transport

Aeroplanes and helicopters are means of **air transport**. Air transport is the fastest way to travel from one place to another. Air travel can be **expensive** and is used to travel to far off places and countries. Aeroplanes carry both passengers and goods.

Aeroplane

Helicopter

expensive: a thing that costs a lot of money

We use different kinds of transport depending on the distance we have to travel, the time we have or the money we want to spend.

Give it a shot

Given below are pictures of some means of transport. Some move slow, some fast and some very fast. Arrange them from slow to fast by numbering them. Write 1 for the slowest vehicle and 10 for the vehicle that moves fastest.

Communication

We communicate with others to give or receive information. We can do this by speaking, writing or using signs and symbols. These are called **means of communication**. Some means of **personal communication** are letters, postcards, greeting cards and telephone. We send letters, postcards and greeting cards to our family and friends by posting them in a letterbox. Nowadays, **modern means of communication** such as mobile phones and emails are used.

We can stay in touch with our family, friends and people we know by communicating with them. We must always be polite while communicating.

Clued in

The telephone was invented by Alexander Graham Bell.

We can call or message people using **telephones** or **mobile phones**. They are the fastest means of communication.

Telephones and mobile phones

We can send and receive a copy of documents through **fax machines**.

Fax machine

We can connect with people anywhere in the world using the **Internet** on **computers**.

Computers

Newspapers tell us what is happening in the country and around the world. They are the cheapest means of communication.

Newspapers

The **radio** is the most common means of communication. People who are unable to read, can listen to the news on the radio.

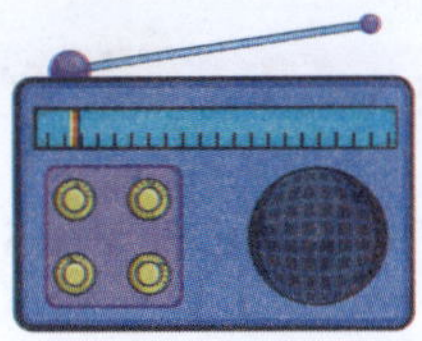

Radio

We can see and hear what is happening in our country and around the world on a **television**.

Television

Mailing a letter

Let us learn how letters reach us.

Posting a letter

Collecting letters

Sorting letters

Delivering a letter

- A letter is dropped into the nearby letterbox.
- A **postman** collects all the letters from the letterbox and takes them to the post office.

- At the post office, the letters are sorted, packed in different mailbags according to the cities and then sent to the receiver's address.
- The letter is delivered by the postman on duty for the area.

Think through

What would happen if you were travelling and could not communicate with your family?

Wrap up

* We use different ways to travel from one place to another.
* Vehicles move on land, on water and in the air.
* Vehicles with engines need fuel to move.
* We communicate with each other using different means of communication.
* Some means of personal communication are letters, postcards, greeting cards and telephone.

Brush up

A Draw a ☺ for the true sentences and a ☹ for the false ones.

1. Travelling became easy after the wheel was invented. ◯
2. All vehicles have an engine. ◯
3. Water transport is the most expensive means of transport. ◯
4. The computer is the fastest means of communication. ◯
5. Radio is the most common means of communication. ◯

B Fill in the blanks with the correct words.

1. A .... is the cheapest means of communication. (telephone/newspaper)
2. A .... and a .... move on land. (bus/helicopter) (car/boat)
3. People send and receive a copy of a letter through .... (television/fax machine)

4. A .... moves on tracks. (metro/plane)
5. Vehicles with engines need .... to move. (animals/fuel)

C Match the following.

1. 	a. Fastest way of travelling
2. 	b. Fastest means of communication
3. 	c. Personal means of communication
4. 	d. Connects people using the Internet
5. 	e. Cheapest means of communication

D Answer these questions.

1. Why do we use different kinds of transport?
2. Why do people travel?
3. Name some means of water transport.

4. How is the mobile phone used for communication?
5. How is the newspaper different from the television as a means of communication?

Learn the ropes

Sometimes, we use signs to communicate with people. Do you know what these signs mean?

Put your heads together

Communication is not just reading and writing. It is also about listening and understanding others. Often we think we hear something but do not understand it. A game called Chinese Whispers, helps us communicate better. Through this game we can learn the importance of listening well. In groups, play this game with your classmates.

Cross connect

Make a paper plane

1. Fold a sheet of paper lengthwise and then open it.
2. Fold the top two corners to meet at the centre line.
3. Fold the new angled edge into the center.
4. Fold along the centre line to hide all folds.
5. Flip the paper over and fold the corners to meet at the centre crease.
6. Fold the wings down on both sides so that they make a straight line from the tip of the plane.

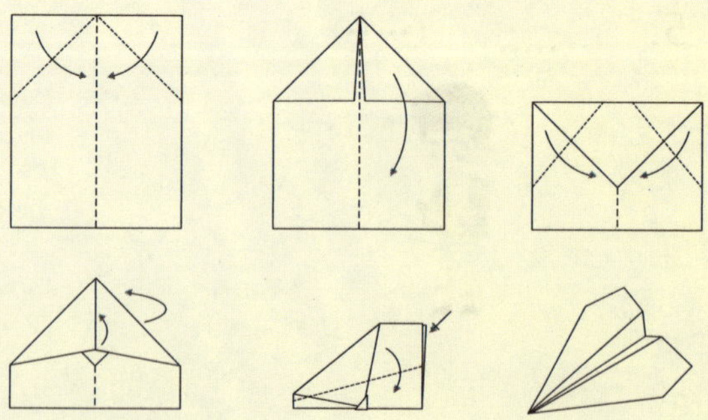

Your paper plane is ready for flight!

17 Directions and Time

Get the ball rolling

How will you explain the way from your classroom to your school library to a person?

While trying to find a new place, we usually ask people for help. They tell us to turn right or left. They might also ask us to move up or down. These are called **directions**. The four main directions are **east**, **west**, **north** and **south**. They help us find places.

The Sun rises in the east. When we stand and look at the rising Sun, we are facing the east. Behind us is the west where the Sun sets. If we stretch our arms, on our left is the north and on our right, is the south. North is **opposite** to the south. East is opposite to the west.

Clued in

We use maps to find places. A map is a drawing of an area on paper. It shows all the places in that area.

opposite: if one thing is opposite another, it is on the other side of it

Left, right, up, down, front or behind are ways of giving simple directions. They are used to find places that are near. To find places that are far away, we use the four main directions. These directions are given on a map too. The top of a map always shows the north and the bottom shows the south. The right of the map shows the east and the left shows the west.

Compass

A **compass** is an object used to find directions. It has a needle that always points to the north.

Give it a shot

Shubham is standing facing the rising Sun outside his house. His house is behind him. On his right is a park and on his left is a tree. Find these places in the picture and write the directions in which they are located.

1. Shubham's house is in the ....
2. The park is in the ....
3. The tree is in the ....
4. Shubham is facing the ....

Time

The position of the Sun in the sky helps us tell time. The period between sunrise to sunset is called **daytime**. When the Sun rises, it is **morning**. When the Sun is directly above our heads, it is 12 o'clock. This time of the day is called **midday** or **noon**.

Morning

Noon

When the Sun sets, it is **evening**. The time between noon and evening is called **afternoon**. The sky turns dark at **night** when the Sun sets completely and we cannot see it. Instead, we see the moon and the stars in the sky. 12 o'clock in the night is called **midnight**. Day and the night together form one complete day.

Evening

Night

Telling Time

We can tell time by looking at a clock, or a watch. Clocks have a **small hand**, a **long hand** and a **thin hand**. The face of the clock also has the digits from 1 to 12. All three hands of the clock move from one number to other. We can count hours, minutes and seconds by looking at these hands. The small hand of the clock tells us the hours, the long hand tells us the minutes, and the thin hand tells us the seconds.

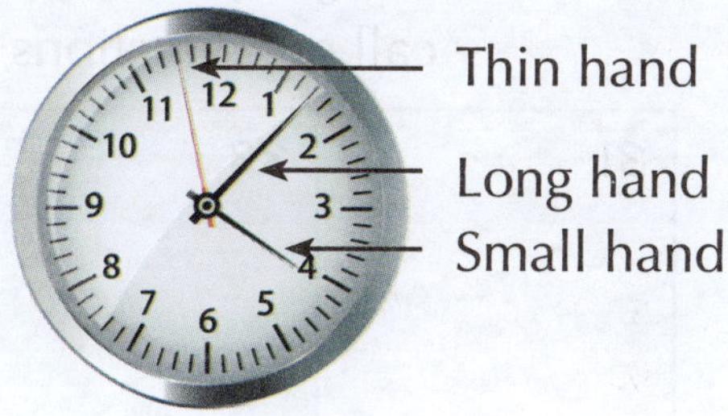

A clock

A complete day is made up of **24 hours**. **Hours** are divided into minutes. **Minutes** are divided into seconds. Each **hour** is made up of **60 minutes**. Each **minute** has **60 seconds** in it.

Weeks, Months and Years

There are **365 days** in a year. A year has **12 months**. Each month is divided into weeks. Each week has **7 days**. There are **52 weeks** in a year.

> **Think through**
>
> Shubham is going to Shimla with his parents for a holiday. They know that they must travel north. They are facing the rising Sun. Which side should they turn to go to Shimla?

Some months of a year have 30 days and some months have 31 days. February has 28 days. Every four years, February has 29 days. This year is called a **leap year**.

We can count the number of days in a month on our hands. Leave out the thumb knuckle. Every month that lands on a knuckle has 31 days. Every month that lands on a groove has 30 days (28 for February).

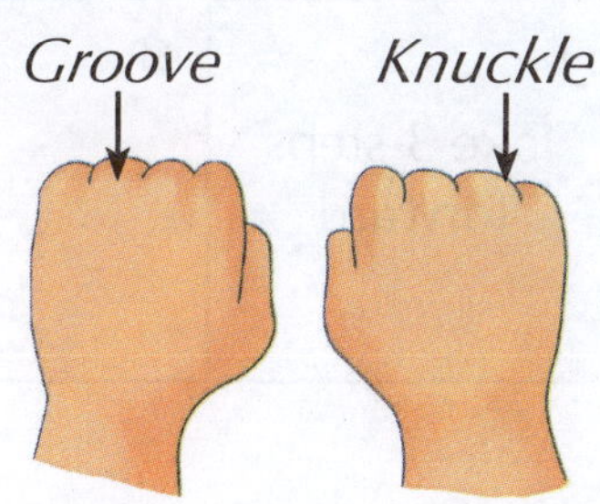

Direction Hopscotch

Let us play direction hopscotch to brush up the four directions. There is one rule of the game—always face the direction of the red arrow. Square 1 is your starting point. To play the game, read the instructions in each square carefully to make your way through the grid. All you have to do is move left, right, forward or backwards. You can trace your path using a pencil or simply by moving your finger over the squares as you move along. To enjoy this game best, you can ask your teacher to draw the grid on the floor and call out directions to you to move or hop from one box to another.

31	32	33 Take three steps to the right	34	35	36 You won!
25	26	27	28	29	30
19 Take one step to the right.	20 Take two steps backward and one step to the left	21	22 Take three steps to the left and one step backward	23	24
13 Take five steps to the right	14	15 Take one step to the right and one step forward	16	17	18 Take one step backward and three steps to the left
7 Take one step forward and two steps to the right	8	9 Take four steps forward	10	11	12
1 Take 3 steps forward START	2	3	4	5	6

↑ Face this direction

Wrap up

- Directions help us to find a place.
- The four main directions are north, south, east and west.
- A map is a drawing of a place on paper.
- A compass is used to find out directions. It has a needle that always points towards the north.
- We can tell the time by looking at a clock or a watch.
- Morning, noon, afternoon, evening and night make up one day.

Brush up

A Draw a ☺ for true sentences and a ☹ for the false ones.

1. Directions help us to find a place.
2. There are four main directions.
3. If we are facing the rising Sun then the north is on our right.
4. A complete day lasts from sunrise to sunset.
5. The long hand of the clock tells us the hours.

B Fill in the blanks.

1. Each minute has .... seconds.
2. There are .... hours in one complete day.
3. A year has .... weeks and .... days.
4. Drawing of a place on paper is called a ....
5. The .... in the sky helps us to tell the time.

C Match the following.

1.	Sunrise	a.	Leap year
2.	Sunset	b.	12 o'clock in night
3.	Short hand	c.	Morning
4.	Midnight	d.	Evening
5.	29 days	e.	Hours

D Answer these questions.

1. Name the four main directions.
2. How can we tell directions by looking at the position of the Sun in the sky?
3. What do the small and long hands of the clock tell us?
4. What is a map?
5. What is noon and midnight?

Learn the ropes

Form groups and find out the directions to your school library, canteen, playground and the teachers' staff room. Find out if these places are to the east, west, north or south of your classroom. Make a list of these places and put up the directions on the soft board.

Put your heads together

Form four groups in class. Each group can select 3 months of the year and make calendars for them using coloured papers. You can mark important holidays and events of each month. Decorate the calendars and put them together. An entire year's calendar for your class is ready!

Cross connect

Shubham learns to play cricket at the cricket academy after school. If his school gets over at 2 p.m. and it takes him one hour to reach the academy, what time will he reach there? Draw a clock showing the time Shubham will reach.

18 Time to Celebrate

Get the ball rolling

Look at the pictures and discuss in class the things you all do while celebrating any festival.

Festivals are special **occasions** we celebrate with our family, relatives, friends and neighbours. During festivals, we meet people, wear new clothes, exchange gifts and sweets, eat special food and enjoy ourselves. Many festivals are celebrated in India. There are three types of festivals. These are **national festivals**, **religious festivals** and **harvest festivals**.

National Festivals

National festivals are celebrated by all Indians. These are days of special importance to the country.

Independence Day is celebrated on 15 August every year. The Prime Minister of India **hoists** the national flag at the Red Fort in Delhi and the **national anthem** is sung.

Independence day

occasion: a special event or celebration; **hoists**: to raise or pull something up to a higher position

Republic Day is celebrated on 26 January every year. The President hoists the national flag. A **parade** is held on Rajpath in New Delhi. The **Rashtrapati Bhavan**, which is the residence of the President of India, is lit in the colours of the national flag.

Republic day

Gandhi Jayanti is celebrated on 2 October. It is the birthday of Mahatma Gandhi. He, along with many other leaders, fought for the independence of India from the British. He is also known as the 'Father of the Nation'.

> **Clued in**
>
> The 25 Indian children who receive the National Bravery Award take part in the Republic Day parade each year.

Religious Festivals

Diwali

People in India celebrate many **religious festivals**.

Diwali is the festival of lights. People clean their houses and decorate them with flowers, lights, candles and *diyas*. They wear new clothes and exchange gifts and sweets with family and friends.

On **Dussehra**, people celebrate the victory of good over evil. **Effigies** of Ravana, his brother and son are burnt all over the country.

Dussehra

Durga Puja is celebrated in West Bengal and all over the country at the same time as Dussehra. People wear new clothes and exchange gifts with their family and friends.

Eid-ul-Fitr

Eid-ul-Fitr is a festival celebrated to mark the end of the month of Ramzan or Ramadan during which people fast. On this day, people wear new clothes and offer special Eid prayers.

parade: people or vehicles moving through a public place to celebrate an important day or event; **effigies**: quickly and roughly made figures

They meet their family and friends and wish them 'Eid Mubarak'. Some people make a special sweet dish called *seviyan* on Eid.

Christmas is celebrated on 25 December every year. People go to church, pray and sing **carols** on Christmas. They decorate their houses and a Christmas tree with lights. They exchange gifts and cakes.

Christmas

Gurpurab

On **Gurpurab**, people celebrate Guru Nanak's birthday. People pray in gurdwaras and eat ***langar*** together.

Harvest Festivals

Harvest festivals are celebrated at the time of **harvest**, when fresh crops are ready to be cut and gathered. People celebrate them all over the country by different names.

Pongal is the harvest festival of Tamil Nadu. It is celebrated every year in January. People decorate their homes with ***rangoli***. A rice **porridge** with milk and jaggery (*gur*) called pongal is made on this day.

Bihu is celebrated in Assam for a good harvest. Special sweet dishes of rice and coconut called *larus* and *pitha* are made. Men and women wear colourful clothes and sing folk songs and dance. Bihu is celebrated in spring, autumn and winter.

Bihu

Onam is a ten-day festival celebrated in Kerala. People decorate elephants and take out **procession**s. Boat races are held and people celebrate the life of King Mahabali. They wear new clothes and decorate their homes with rangolis.

carols: songs that are sung on Christmas; **langar**: when free food is given in a gurdwara; **harvest**: the time of year when the crops are gathered in a farm; **rangoli**: making patterns on floor with petals or sand or powder for decoration; **porridge**: a thick sticky food made from oats; **procession:** a huge group of people that moves along slowly

Lohri

Lohri is celebrated every year in January in many parts of India especially Delhi, Punjab and Haryana. People celebrate this festival by lighting **bonfires**. Lohri is celebrated with popcorn, rice flakes and jaggery or gur.

Think through

Why should we celebrate all festivals?

Everyone enjoys celebrating festivals. People of different religions join in the celebration of all the festivals spreading joy and togetherness.

Give it a shot

Read the clues and name these festivals.

1. We light candles and diyas.

....

2. We are going for a boat race.

....

3. I am going with my family to have langar.

....

4. I am making rangoli and mom is making rice porridge.

....

5. I am on a fast and am going to pray.

....

6. I am putting popcorn and rice flakes in the bonfire.

....

bonfires: a fire that is made outdoors

Wrap up

- Festivals are special occasions which we celebrate with our family, relatives, friends and neighbours.
- We meet each other, wear special clothes, exchange gifts and sweets, eat special food and enjoy ourselves during festivals.
- In India, we celebrate three kinds of festivals—national festivals, religious festivals and harvest festivals.

Brush up

A **Fill in the blanks using the words in the box.**

Independence Day	Republic Day	Onam	Pongal	Bihu

1. .... is a harvest festival of Tamil Nadu.
2. Elephants are decorated during the festival of ....
3. Every year .... is celebrated on 15 August.
4. .... is a national festival that is celebrated in January.
5. In Assam, men and women wear colourful sarees and sing and dance during ....

B **Match the following.**

1. Eid-ul-Fitr	a. Mahatma Gandhi
2. Christmas	b. Langar
3. Gandhi Jayanti	c. Seviyan
4. Gurpurab	d. Christmas tree
5. Diwali	e. Festivals of lights

C **Draw a 🙂 for true sentences and a ☹ for false ones.**

1. Lohri is celebrated by lighting bonfires ◯
2. Durga Puja is celebrated in Assam. ◯

3. On Dussehra, people celebrate the victory of good over evil.

4. Eid-ul-Fitr marks the end of the month of Ramadan.

5. Onam is celebrated thrice a year.

D **Answer these questions.**

1. Name two religious festivals.
2. Why is Gandhi Jayanti a national festival?
3. Who hoists the national flag on the Independence Day and where?
4. Why do we celebrate harvest festivals?
5. How is Pongal celebrated?

Learn the ropes

Earth Day is celebrated on 22 April every year. It reminds everyone that the Earth needs to be saved. How do you think this day should be celebrated?

Put your heads together

Holi is celebrated in March every year. In groups, find out if Holi is a religious, national or harvest festival. Collect pictures of people from all parts of India celebrating it and make a collage on a chart paper. Paste pictures of the special sweets made during this festival.

Cross connect

Make your Festival Calendar.

- Find out the dates of all the important festivals of a year.
- Write the names of the festivals along with the dates and paste pictures related to them.
- Pin up the Festival Calendar in your room.

19 Clothes We Wear

Get the ball rolling

Do you wear different clothes for different occasions? Which is your favourite dress?

We wear clothes to protect ourselves from heat, rain, cold, sun and insects. Different clothes are worn during different seasons. **Summer**, **winter** and the **rainy season** are the three main seasons in India.

Summer Clothes

In India, it is very hot in the summer, so the clothes we wear are made from **cotton** or **linen**. We get cotton and linen from plants. Clothes made from them are light and keep our body cool.

Frock

T-Shirt

Skirt

Shorts

Winter Clothes

It is cold in the winter. We wear **woollen** clothes that keep us warm. We also wear warm clothes when we go to the mountains.

Sweater

Cap, muffler, gloves

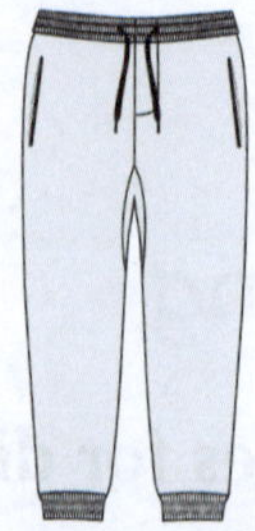
Woollen pants

Coat

We get **wool** from the body hair of sheep and rabbits. Camel hair is also used to make warm clothes. In winter, we also wear clothes made of **silk**. We get silk from **silkworms**. They live in a **cocoon** made of long threads. Silk is obtained from these threads.

Silkworm and cocoons

We get wool from a sheep

Clued in

Men too wear skirts! In Scotland, men wear skirts called kilts.

Leather is used to make purses, bags, shoes, sandals, wallets, belts and jackets. Leather is made from the skin of snakes and crocodiles and some other animals. The fur on the body of some animals is also used to make coats and jackets. However, the use of fur is now strictly banned. We should try to avoid buying things that are made by killing animals.

Clothes for Rainy Season

During the rainy season, we wear **waterproof** clothes like raincoats and gumboots. They are made from rubber, nylon or plastic. We carry umbrellas to keep our clothes from getting wet.

Raincoat

Gumboots

Umbrella

cocoon: a covering of silk threads that some insects make to protect themselves before they become adults; **waterproof**: material that does not let water through

Special Clothes

People wear special clothes to work, on weddings and festivals. Do you wear particular type of clothes to school? These are called **uniforms**. Some professionals also wear uniforms depending on the work they do.

We go to school wearing uniforms

We also wear special clothes during special **occasions** like parties and marriages. People wear different types of clothes on their weddings.

Different types of wedding clothes

Give it a shot

Look at the uniforms of some professionals and complete their names.

1. P .... C E O .... I C ....

2. N .... R .... E

3. P .... T

4. S .... D .... T

5. .... O C .... R

6. F .... F I G ....

occasions: a particular time something happens

Many countries have a special dress called the **national dress**. These are traditional dresses of a particular country. Saree is one of the most popular dresses of India.

Sometimes we wear special clothes for swimming, acting in a play, for dancing or performing on stage. These clothes are called **costumes**. We also wear costumes on special events like the annual day in school.

A woman wearing a saree

A dancer's costume

It is important that the clothes we wear are washed, cleaned and ironed. Wearing clean clothes keeps us healthy.

Think through

What is the name of the national dress of Japan?

Wrap up

* Clothes are worn according to the season and the place we live in.
* We wear clothes made of cotton in the summer and clothes made of wool or silk in winter.
* During the rainy season, we wear raincoats and gumboots made of plastic, rubber or nylon.
* Some people need to wear uniforms to work just as students wear uniform to school.
* Many countries have a special dress called the national dress.
* Clothes worn for a special purpose are called costumes.

Brush up

A Fill in the blanks.

1. Clothes protect us from ...., ... and ....
2. In summer, we wear clothes made from .... and ....
3. In winter, we wear clothes from made from .... and ....

4. School students wear a .... to school.
5. Dancers on stage wear a ....

B Match the following.

1.	Linen	a.	Uniform
2.	Wool	b.	Summer
3.	Gumboots	c.	Winter
4.	Pilot	d.	Rainy season

C Write three different types of clothes we wear that are made from these things.

1. Cotton .... , ... , ...
2. Silk .... , ... , ...
3. Rubber .... , ... , ...
4. Wool .... , ... , ...

D Answer these questions.

1. Why should we wear cotton clothes in summer?
2. Where do we get wool from?
3. Why should we wear clothes made from wool in winter?
4. Name three types of people who need to wear uniforms.
5. How is a uniform different from a costume?

Learn the ropes

What do you do with the clothes that do not fit you anymore? Have you given your clothes to your younger brother or sister to wear? Who else can you give these clothes to? You must not give torn clothes to anyone.

Put your heads together

In groups, find out the national dresses of five countries. On a world map, paste their pictures on the countries to which they belong. Write the name of the dresses below the pictures.

Cross connect

When we go to the market to buy clothes, the shopkeeper asks us the size. Find out the size of your shirt, shorts or any other types of clothes you wear and write them in the table.

Clothes	Size
T-Shirt	
Shirt	
Jeans	
Shorts	
Shoes	

20 Safety Rules

Get the ball rolling

Do you take care when you are on road? Look at these pictures. Discuss them in class.

Safety means being safe from any kind of danger. **Accidents** happen when we are **careless**. They can cause serious injuries. Following safety rules keeps us from getting hurt. We should follow safety rules at home, in school, on the road and inside vehicles.

Safety Rules at Home

We should never play with sharp objects like knives, scissors, blades and compass.

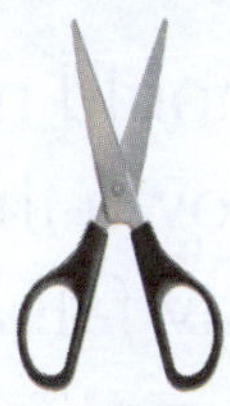

Scissors

Paper cutter

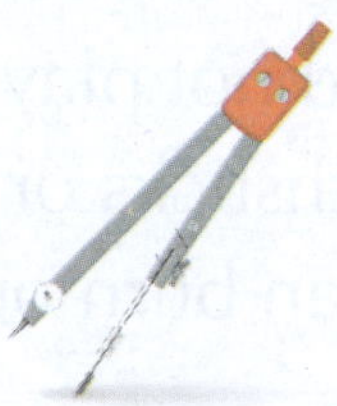

Compass

careless: not paying enough attention to what we are doing

We should not touch switches and electric **gadgets** like an iron, kettle, oven or a toaster with wet hands.

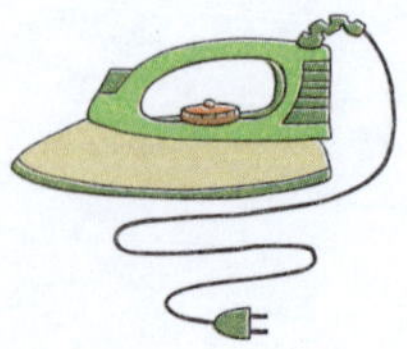

Iron

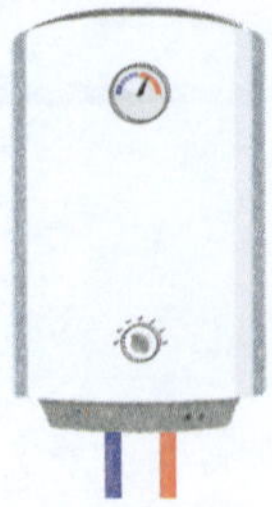

Geyser

Toaster

Oven

We should not touch wires or electric sockets.

We should never play with medicines or taste them.

We should put our toys back in their place after playing, else we might step on them and fall.

We should not play with matchsticks or light them. It can burn our fingers.

We should not play in the kitchen or near a gas stove or touch hot pan or hot water.

We should not run up and down the stairs, as we may fall and hurt ourselves.

gadgets: small machines or devices that do something useful

Safety Rules at School

We should not climb on desks and chairs in class. We might fall and hurt ourselves.

While playing on swings, we should never push each other. We should stand away from the swing while waiting for our turn.

We should always walk in a **queue**. We should not push or hit others.

Give it a shot

Write the safety rules of your school on a chart paper. Then pin it on the bulletin board of your classroom.

Safety Rules on the Road

We should be very careful on roads.

- We should always walk on the road with an adult and never alone.
- We should always hold the hands of an adult while walking on a **pavement**, or while crossing the road.
- We should always cross the road at a **zebra crossing** with an adult.
- We should never play or run on the road.
- If someone gets hurt we must give them **first aid**.

Never cross the road alone

queue: a line of people or vehicles that are waiting for something; **pavement**: a path with a hard surface, usually by the side of a road

First Aid

First aid is the **immediate** help given to an injured or a sick person. If the person is not hurt badly, basic first aid helps.

Some First Aid Tips

- Call an adult or a doctor immediately when you see an injured person or a person who needs help.
- Do not allow people to crowd around a person who is hurt.
- Try to calm down the injured person.
- Give the person water to drink.

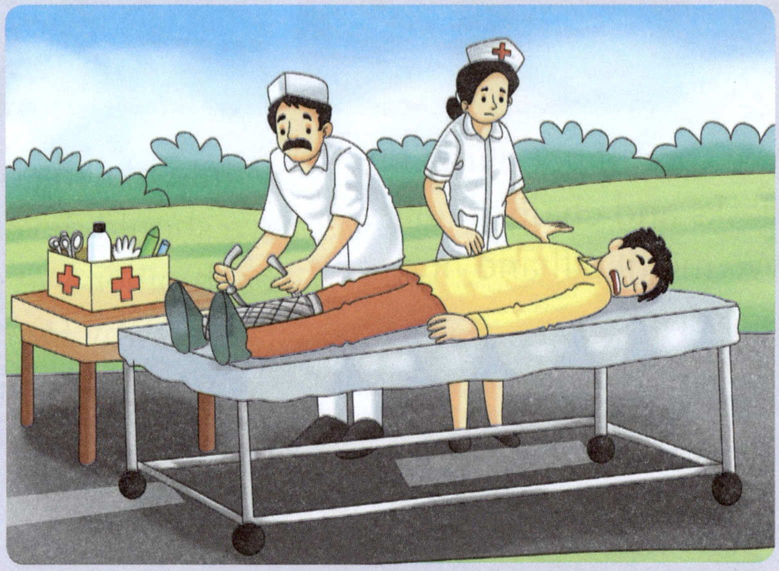

Giving first aid

First Aid Kit

The **first aid kit** contains things necessary for a **basic medical treatment**. A first aid kit has the following things:

- Cotton wool
- Bandages
- Crepe bandage
- Thermometer
- Antiseptic cream or lotion
- Ointment for pain
- Cold pack
- A pair of scissors
- A pair of tweezers

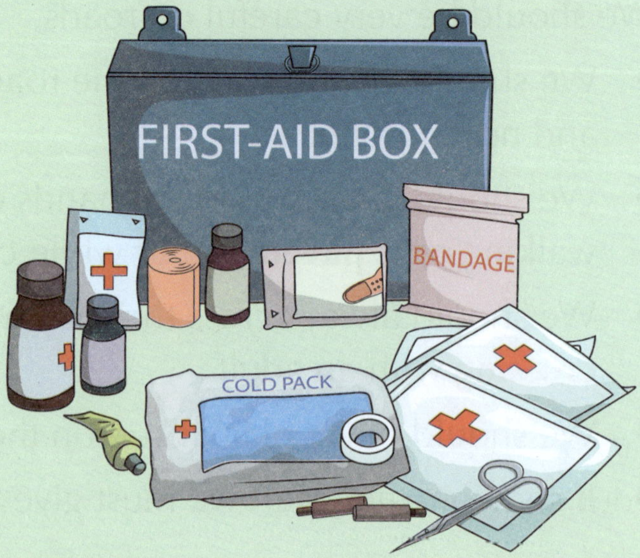

immediate: an action that happens very quickly

Safety Rules Inside Vehicles

We should wait in a queue at a bus stop. We should not push others while **boarding** the bus. We should wait for the bus to stop before boarding or getting off.

Think through

What will you do if any of your friends fall while getting off a bus?

We should board the bus in a queue.

We should always wear a seat belt while sitting in a car. We should never try to open the door of a moving vehicle.

Clued in

Cycling tracks are made for people who ride bicycles on the road. We should always cycle on these tracks to be safe.

We should never put our hand or head out of the moving vehicle.

Never scream in a moving bus as it may disturb the driver and lead to an accident.

boarding: to get on a vehicle to travel somewhere

Wrap up

* Safety means being safe from any kind of danger.
* To keep ourselves safe, we should follow all the safety rules.
* First aid is the immediate help given to a sick or injured person.

Brush up

A Match the following.

1. 
2. 
3. 
4. 

a. Safety at home b. Safety in school c. Safety in a vehicle d. Safety on the road

B Fill in the blanks with the correct answers.

1. We should not touch .... with wet hands. (wires/towels)
2. .... means staying safe from any kind of danger. (Accident/Safety)
3. We should always .... away from the swing. (stand/sleep)
4. .... aid is the immediate help given to a person who is sick or injured. (Second/First)
5. We should always .... in a line. (walk/jump)

C Draw a ☺ for true sentences and a ☹ for false ones.

1. We should try to open the door of the moving vehicle. ◯
2. We should wait for our turn and not push each other on slides or swings. ◯

3. We should not play with matchsticks as they might burn our fingers.

4. We should not play with sharp objects.

5. We should play in the kitchen or near a gas stove.

D Answer these questions.

1. Write three safety rules that we should follow on the road.
2. How can we avoid accidents at home?
3. What are the two important rules you should follow when you are inside vehicle?
4. What is first aid?

Learn the ropes

How will you help an elderly person walking on a road?

Put your heads together

Form four groups. Each group should make a poster about one of these topics – safety rules at home, safety rules at school, safety rules on roads and safety rules inside vehicles. Draw pictures and make the posters colourful.

Cross connect

1. Form groups and enact safety rules as a play.
2. Recite a poem about safety rules.

Dance Forms of India

Different states of India have different dance forms.

Kathak

Kathak is dance form of northern India. It originated in northern India, mainly in Varanasi and Lucknow. Kathak comes from the word *Katha*, which means 'a story'. The Kathak dancers tell a story through their dance.

Manipuri

The Manipuri dance or *Raas lila* is known for its beautiful costumes and the soft, gentle music and dance movements. It originated in the state of Manipur.

Odissi

Odissi is the dance form of Odisha. It is a temple dance performed mainly by women. Religious stories are told through this dance.

Bhangra

Bhangra is one of the most popular folk dances from Punjab. Beats of the drum, lots of energy and feet movement are some features of this dance. The dancers wear brightly-coloured *lungis* and turbans.

Kuchipudi

Kuchipudi is the dance form of Andhra Pradesh. It is one of the oldest dance forms of India. It involves telling a story through beautiful stage and feet movements.

Dandiya

Another folk dance full of energy is the Dandiya from Gujarat. This dance is performed with sticks or *dandiyas*, which represent the swords of the Goddess Durga. It is widely performed during the Navaratri puja. Women wear colourful *ghagra* and *choli* that have tiny mirrors sewn on them. The men wear *kedias* and turbans.

Bharatanatyam

Bharatanatyam is one of the most famous dances of India. It originated in the states of Tamil Nadu and Karnataka. The Bharatanatyam dance form has four beautiful elements—**expression**, beat, music and dance. Brightly-coloured silk sarees are worn as the costume for this dance.

Ghoomar

This folk dance from Rajasthan originated in the Bhil tribe of the state. The name of dance means to **twirl** or *ghoomna* in Hindi. The dance has several twirling motions by the dancers. The women dancers wear colourful ghagras with dupattas covering their faces.

expression: to say, write or do something in order to express your feelings; **twirl:** to dance round and round

Staying Safe

A 'pandemic' is when a disease spreads from person to person throughout the world. We must keep ourselves safe during a pandemic.

Follow these rules to stay safe:

Don't touch your nose, mouth, eyes with dirty hands. Use a handkerchief when coughing and sneezing.

During COVID, hand hygiene helps save lives—wash hands and stay clean!

Use a mask when stepping out during the pandemic.

Maintain social distancing when you go out.

SOCIAL DISTANCING

Colour these pictures and follow these steps to wash your hands.

WASH YOUR HANDS

1
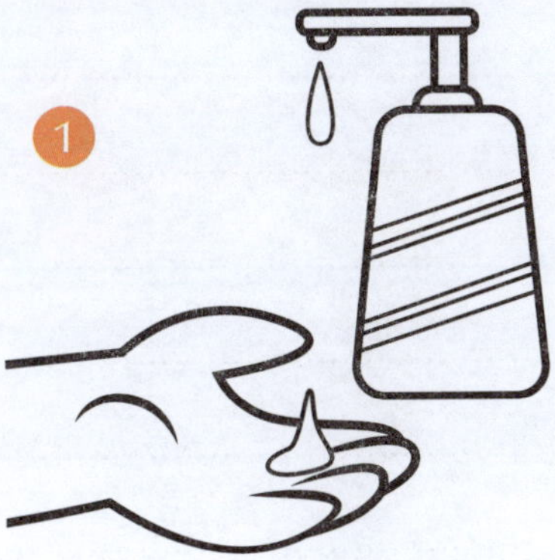
Use soap

2
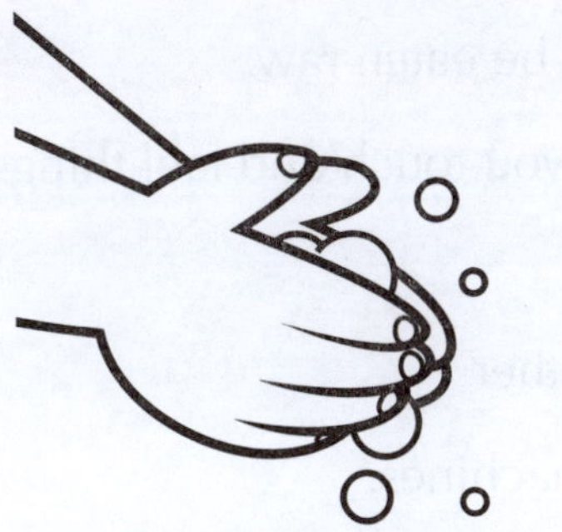
Rub palm to palm

3

Rub the back of your hands

4

Interlace your fingers

5

Clean the base of your thumb

6
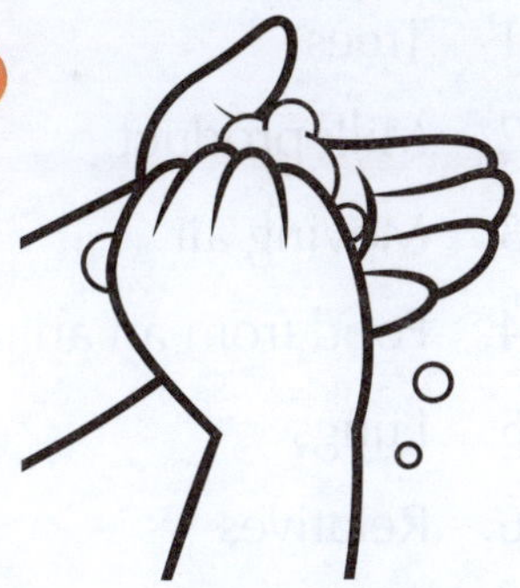
Clean your fingernails

7

Rub your wrists

8
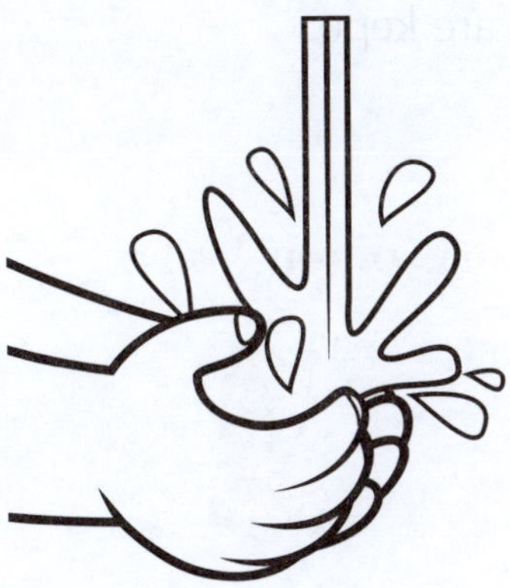
Rinse your hands

9
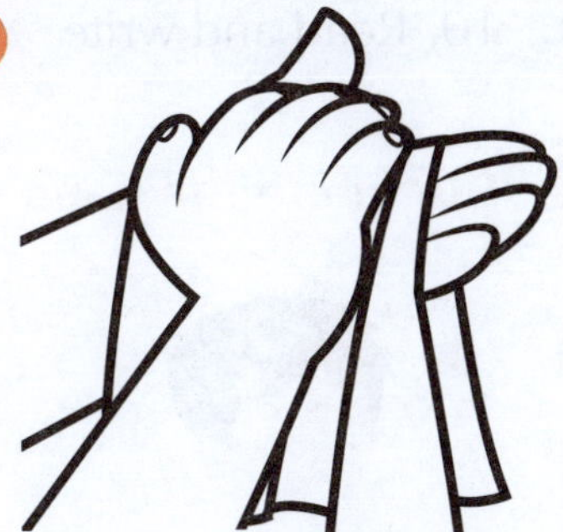
Dry your hands

Suggested Assessment 1

A Guess who am I? Use the words given in the box.

carrot	oxygen	lab assistant	seed	skin	uncle	rain	honeybee	brain	engineer

1. I have a baby plant inside me. ....
2. I help you to think and collect information. ....
3. I am the main source of water. ....
4. I am a gas, I come from trees and help you breathe. ....
5. I am a vegetable which can be eaten raw. ....
6. I am a sense organ; I make you touch and feel things. ....
7. I make honey and wax. ....
8. I am the brother of your mother. ....
9. I build roads, bridges and machines. ....
10. I look after the computers in school. ....

B Match the following.

1. Trees	a. Library
2. Milk product	b. Family members
3. Moving air	c. Profession
4. Food from an animal	d. Principal
5. Lungs	e. Teachers
6. Relatives	f. Oxygen
7. Work for which people are trained	g. Egg
8. Head of the school	h. Butter
9. A place where many books are kept	i. Breathe
10. Read and write	j. Wind

C Complete the names of the parts of our body.

1. H .... A ......

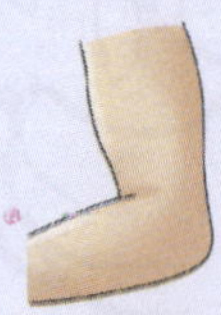

2. E .... O W

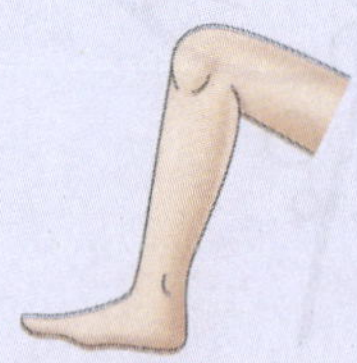

3. K .... E ....

Suggested Assessment 2

A **Draw a 🙂 for true sentences and a ☹ for false ones.**

1. Gandhi Jayanti is a religious festival.
2. Vehicles with engines run on fuel.
3. Food items that make our bones and muscles strong are called energy-giving food.
4. Trains that carry people are called passenger trains.
5. A person who sells things in a shop is called a chemist.
6. When wind moves very fast, it is called a storm.
7. Pucca houses can be moved from one place to another.
8. Wild animals choose to live in places where they get plenty of food.
9. The top of a map always shows the south.
10. Water from the tap is not fit for drinking.

B **Circle the answers in the word grid with the help of the clues given below.**

N	E	I	G	H	B	O	U	R	S
D	S	A	F	E	T	Y	K	I	F
I	L	U	N	I	V	E	R	S	E
W	E	A	T	H	E	R	I	L	S
A	P	A	R	T	I	N	S	A	T
L	T	R	A	C	K	S	A	N	I
I	G	L	O	O	S	P	R	D	V
C	O	M	P	A	S	S	E	B	A
M	E	A	T	H	E	R	E	O	L

Clues:

1. Being safe from danger
2. A popular dress of India
3. Special occasions celebrated with family, relatives and friends
4. This can be sunny, foggy, rainy, cloudy or windy
5. An object used to find directions
6. A train moves on these
7. The festival of lights
8. An area of land surrounded with water
9. Sun, moon, stars and the Earth are part of this
10. Houses made of snow
11. Families or people who live in houses next to and near our house

C Draw a diya and a Christmas tree.